WATERLOO HIGH SCHOOL LIBRARY
1464 INDUSTRY RD.
ATWATER, OHIO 44201

W9-ANW-321

WATERLOO HIGH SCHOOL LIBRARY
1464 INDUSTRY RD.
ATWATER, OHIO 44201

HOW TO MAKE YOUR OWN FURNITURE

How to Make Your Own Furniture

BY

HENRY LIONEL WILLIAMS

AVENEL BOOKS · NEW YORK

684
wiL

Copyright © MCMLI by Henry Lionel Williams
All rights reserved.
This edition is published by Avenel Books
a division of Barre Publishing Company, Inc.
by arrangement with the author
Manufactured in the United States Of America

u t s r q p o n

Design and Typography by Elaine C. Farrar

CONTENTS

A. MOVABLE FURNITURE

Sconce

Pipe Box

Hanging Bookshelf

Standing Bookshelf

Cutlery Tray

Spice Box Lamp Base

Sawbuck Coffee Table

Lamp Table

Trestle Dining Table

Drop Leaf Table

Hutch Table

Modern Tray Table

Joint Stool

Loose-Seat Stool

Five-Board Bench

Side Chair and Arm Chair

Wing Chair

Chaise Longue

Modern Bedstead

Low-Post Bedstead

Tall-Post Bedstead

Welsh Dresser

Chest of Drawers

Framed Desk

Corner Cupboard

B. BUILT-IN FURNITURE

Recessed Bookshelf Cupboard

Corner Cupboard

Door-Flanking Bookcase

Three-Unit Counter and Cupboard

Closet and Dressing Table Alcove

Corner Seat

Closet — Bunk — Desk

Double Bunks, Detached or Attached

Divan with Drawers

Cabinet Table for Corner Beds

Twin Beds with Bookshelf-Desk

Sofa with Bookcase and End Tables

Wall Angle Cabinet

Corner Counter with Drop Table

Bathroom, Kitchen or Bar Counter

HOW TO MAKE YOUR OWN FURNITURE

Setting Up Shop

Chapter I

Setting Up Shop

There are few occupations for pleasure or profit, as satisfying as working in wood. And this satisfaction is nowhere more fully realized than in shaping wood into things of beauty and utility that add charm and comfort to the home.

The material itself is pleasant to handle and easy to work; it is clean and tractable, and almost anyone with the slightest mechanical aptitude can acquire, without too much difficulty, the necessary skill. Such is the appeal of cabinet making, and the reason why so many take to furniture construction as a hobby or even turn it into a business.

It is unfortunate that many amateur cabinet makers, in their haste to finish jobs they have started, lose sight of the basic essentials of good workmanship—patience and care. They need to learn that the fullest satisfaction comes only to the conscientious craftsman to whom good workmanship is a prime essential. To the amateur who make that his ideal the rest will be easy. The beginner does not need skill so much as a capacity for taking pains. If he learns to exercise care, skill will come soon enough.

Equally important is a capacity to appreciate good design. After he has examined and studied and made himself familiar with really good furniture, the serious craftsman is seldom interested in the simple knick-knacks or the ugly and rubbishy gewgaws that tempt so many enthusiastic but misguided and impatient beginners. The serious worker

2

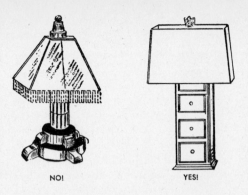

NO!   YES!

edges. He would certainly enclose the space below the bottom shelf, and perhaps cut the skirt into a decorative shape. This base would have the effect of giving four feet to the cabinet, and allow it to stand more firmly on the floor.

The difference between the two jobs therefore would not be one of extra skill on the part of the professional, but of a practical application of a knowledge of design and the way these things are usually done for the best results. The closed-in base, as can readily be seen, is better from every standpoint. It shuts off a space that would collect dust yet be too low to permit of its being swept out. Thus for very little extra expenditure of labor and material a much more impressive and expensive-looking job results.

knows that these elementary exercises are a waste of time that could better be devoted to producing furniture pieces that are not only useful but well-designed and in good taste.

The beginner needs to realize that the difference between an amateur-looking and a professional job, though important, is very small. Often it is merely a matter of a piece of moulding or a corner brace, or a little extra sanding of the end grain.

In making a simple bedside lampstand and bookcase, for example, the tyro probably would be content with finishing everything off flush, and running the sides down to form feet. The professional, on the other hand, would give the top a slight overhang and form a simple thumb moulding on three

This principle can be extended to all kinds of furniture and cabinet-making jobs, including the selection of tools and the care they receive after they have been acquired. The professional gets the best tools he can afford, and buys at the same time all the equipment necessary to keep them in first-class working condition. There is no reason why any beginner, amateur or hobbyist, cannot do the same. All that is required is that high standards be set in the beginning—and adhered to throughout.

It is for these serious-minded amateurs that this book is written, and they will find that it is just as

POOR
(AMATEUR)

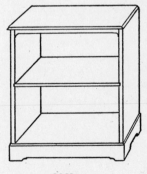

GOOD
(PROFESSIONAL)

easy, and far more rewarding, to make good furniture and accessories as it is to waste valuable time and material on junk. Of course, to the man starting his shop as a business, quality will be the first consideration anyway; it is the best means he can use to meet competition.

Insofar as built-in pieces are concerned—and their consideration occupies a considerable portion of this volume—there is always a temptation to skimp in detail on parts that are not seen—perhaps on the theory that the walls of the house will keep it from falling apart. But this is not good practice, for either the furniture or its maker; sloppy habits once acquired are hard to break. Where cabinet-making and carpentering practices are combined—as in the case of built-ins—the tendency should always be toward the more careful work.

The man who constructs built-in pieces in his home should consider first and last that a job well designed and well done will add to the cash value of his house and make it more salable, as well as give him added pride in his home. Poor workmanship and design can have just the opposite effect.

The amount of space available for the workshop and the quality and quantity of tools that can be acquired will determine to a large extent the type and size, and perhaps intricacy, of the pieces that can be turned out—but limiting factors should not influence quality.

The first thing to aim for is excellence of workmanship through painstaking effort. In this, the tools play a large part. Good tools last longer and help in doing good work—provided they are kept in good shape. If the worker purchases good tools he will be more likely to take proper care of them than if he buys cheap ones. The beginner should buy the best tools he can afford.

If it is necessary to deal with large pieces of wood, room will be required to work on them from either end. Sometimes a small room with strategically placed doors or windows—through which to poke the free end of a long piece—will serve just as well as a bigger room. But it is much better not to have to rely on such borrowed space, especially in bad weather.

If there are one or more power tools, it is well to have them movable so that large pieces can be fed to them from either side. This means a sufficiently long electric cord (or alternative outlets) and a solid base for the tool that does not need to be fastened to the floor. Usually, the tool that benefits most from this arrangement is the bench saw. In any case, before installing either bench- or floor-type tools and equipment, it is wise to make a scale plan of the room (of at least half an inch to the foot), and cut out pieces of cardboard to the same scale to represent the tools, etc. Then by shifting the pieces around they can be located efficiently. The locations of doors and windows should be considered.

Other prime requisites of working space are plenty of light and comfortable working temperature in all seasons. The space needed will be governed to some extent to the kind of work to be done and the size of the pieces to be handled. If the purpose is to confine attention to small gadgets such as wall boxes and hanging bookshelves, very little elbow room beyond the bench surface will be needed—provided there are no power tools to take up floor space.

For lighting, nothing can beat daylight—and if that can't be arranged for, or if the shop must be used before and after daylight hours, the best substitute undoubtedly is the fluorescent light. It may cost more than an ordinary fixture but it will soon save the cost through smaller electricity bills. However, just any kind of fluorescent lamps will not do —especially in shop concerned with colors and finishing. The lamps must give the closest approach to daylight that can be had. This can be checked by looking at paint color cards, first in daylight then by the light of the lamps. The so-called "white"

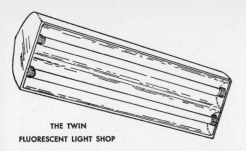

**THE TWIN
FLUORESCENT LIGHT SHOP**

tube usually is much too pink, and the "daylight" tube much too blue. A combination of the two will give much better results—or at least the colors applied under such a light will look more natural in daylight.

To get good fluorescent distribution requires large lamps with long tubes (and two tubes to a fixture—which, incidentally, reduces flicker), or two fixtures to a tool so that there is no shadow on one side. The 40-watt tubes, four feet long, are ideal in many cases, but sufficient of them must be used to give adequate lighting over all working spaces and machines, without shadows. For a power drill or jigsaw a supplementary spotlight will be called for, focused on the work and usually attached to the machine itself. These can be the ordinary type of light bulb, but they should have a shade so that the light is concentrated on the work and does not get in the operator's eyes.

Equally as important as unhampered vision is bodily comfort—for which the first requisite is proper working temeprature. Frozen fingers are no aid to good work, and neither is perspiration in the eyes. It is essential also to have a comfortable floor to stand on. Concrete may be cool and clean, but it is also tiring. Usually, something a little more resilient is called for—a wooden boarded floor is perhaps best. It has the necessary "give" and has insulating value against heat and cold.

If there is a concrete floor, the best thing to do is to make a few platforms to stand on in the most-used working spaces. These should be as low as they can be without eliminating the "spring", and have a solid base all around so that one will not be tripped by catching his toes under overhanging edges. If the space can be afforded to bevel off the edges into miniature ramps, so much the better. Safety is of paramount importance in any shop, large or small, and it may often depend on such apparently unimportant details. A solid-topped platform is better than a duckboard because tools and other things dropped are more readily noticed and recovered if there are no spaces for them to fall through.

Accidents will occasionally happen in the best-regulated shops. Even expert users of edged tools occasionally gash their fingers, so it does not pay to ignore the humble Bandaid. A box of simple first-aid equipment should be kept handy—adhesive tape, scissors to cut it, and three sizes of roller bandages ($\frac{1}{2}$, $1\frac{1}{2}$, and 2-in.), an assortment of band-aids, a small package of absorbent cotton, and a half-ounce bottle of iodine. Learn how and when to apply these—then let everyone do his best to avoid having to use any of them, by keeping his mind on what he is doing and by taking his time.

In setting up the first shop, cost may often be a prime consideration to the beginner. Fortunately here are many operations that can be done by hand almost as well as they can by machine—provided the worker has the requisite time and patience. Actually it is good training for both the hand and eye to do things with hand tools. Furthermore, in making reproductions of old-time pieces of furniture it is possible to give them a much more authentic look and feel if at least the final operations are done without the aid of power tools. Lines can be too straight, and edges too unswerving, while certain slight and natural imperfections may give the piece charm just because they recall the days before the machine was king. Even some modern designs would benefit from evidences of hand work, so it is better not to be too anxious to mechanize the shop in the beginning. A good range of high-quality tools will provide a sounder introduction to this ancient and honorable craft.

On the other hand, when a shop is being operated for profit, power tools are indispensable. If the operator is to make a living from his work, time is certainly money, and only power equipment will enable him to cash in on that fact. Even with hand-finished work, the initial cutting out and shaping can usually be done by machine with no noticeable effect on the final product insofar as appearance is concerned.

Therefore, in setting up shop, the logical procedure is first to estimate the cost of the essentials, then balance that against the available funds. This will reveal how much there is on hand for power equipment and other labor-saving devices. These points are dealt with in detail in Chapter II. The final decisions on shop equipment will depend largely on the type of work it is proposed to do, whether it is for fun or for profit, and, if the latter, the kind of market it is intended to seek. In either case there are a number of things that it is possible to have done outside—if there is no objection to paying the price.

Wood can be got in the rough and cut up and planed in the shop, or the mill will plane it and cut it to size. This is often a consideration where the operator of a small shop uses thin wood—say half-inch or less. A planer is a costly machine, and few small shops can afford one or provide enough work to justify its purchase. In such cases it pays to have the material supplied in the finished dimensions. This might also happen when a large number of pieces of lumber of the same dimensions are needed. These are all things to consider in embarking on any serious shop project.

The beginner bent on making more ambitious furniture such as upholstered pieces—stools, chairs, love-seats, etc., should remember that upholstering is a business in itself, and few one-man woodworking shops can afford to embark upon it. This should be borne in mind when planning projects.

All in all, the physical problems of equipping and operating a small shop are few and simple—unless it is to be established on a strictly business basis, whereupon a certain amount of business acumen and selling ability need to be added to skill with tools and an appreciation of good design. That phase of the subject, however, is outside the province of this book. Here we are concerned simply with showing the reader how to make good furniture, either portable or built-in, that he will be proud to own and find easy to sell.

Tools and Equipment

Chapter II

Tools and Equipment

Workbench and Accessories

Bench. Of all the equipment necessary to the cabinet shop, the most important undoubtedly is the bench. Even in shops equipped with power tools here is where the actual fitting is done and the final touches put upon the parts as they are finished and assembled. Here, too, much of the marking, cutting, and planing is done, as well as the regular hand operations. The bench must be designed, located, and equipped with this in mind.

Actually, you don't usually need a great deal of working space. For most purposes a bench top 5 feet long and 15 inches wide provides all the level space you will need. Behind this 15-inch-wide top you can have either a level or a sunken space of

7½ inches or so, finished by a backboard either with or without a rack for tools attached to its top edge. Your bench will thus be 60" x 22½" overall. Many cabinet makers use a bench six inches shorter than this.

The bench height should be gauged to suit your own height. On an average, the bench top height should be between 30 and 33 inches so that work held in the vise, or laid on the bench, can be placed with a minimum of strain and effort.

Of course there will always be occasions on which the bench height will not be suitable. Our own solution of this problem is to keep under the bench a pair of platforms, one 3 inches high and the other 5 inches high. The higher one is 4 feet 2 inches long and the low one 6 inches shorter so that it slides under its big brother, and both go under the bench when not in use. In this way you can readily increase your own height to deal with wide boards and bulky pieces, and so maintain a comfortable and easy working position. But make the platforms so light that you can drag them out with the toe of your shoe instead of stooping and groping.

The bench top should be perfectly stiff and rigid, so you need two 8" x 60" planks (finished to 7½"), at least 1¾" and preferably 2" thick. This should be of some hard wood such as maple or oak. At the rear of this heavy top you will have a 1" x 8" board (¾" x 7½" finished), also laid flat. The difference in thickness between the planks and the board will give you a trough or recess. Into this you can push aside tools, screws, and other small objects while you are getting the work ready to use them. A lone screw can wreak awful damage if you lay the finished side of a board on it.

Behind the trough will be your vertical backboard. This can be level with the working surface or several inches higher to support a tool rack or shelf.

All of these parts are mounted on a frame comprised of four 3" x 3" legs into which are tenoned two longitudinal 3 x 3's (one back, one front) 6 inches from the bottom. There will also be four transverse 3 x 3's (two at each end), one at the top of the legs, the other 9 inches from the bottom.

This frame is made 6 inches shorter than the top planks so that when the top is attached it overlaps the frame by 3 inches at each end. This 3 inches gives a place to which you can clamp work when necessary—a very useful provision. Since there is no vertical board or apron under the front edge of the top you can use that for clamping also. This means that if you install a drawer under the top you will have to set it back about 2 inches.

The advantage of having a drawer in the workbench is debatable. Such a drawer is useful if you have no other place to store certain tools, or wish to lock them up when not in use. Otherwise it can be a terrible nuisance groping for tools in a drawer that has to be opened—and closed again—when the bench is in use. Ordinarily, it is far better to have all tools where you can see and reach them, but if you *must* have a drawer in the bench let it be a shallow one and not a bottomless catch-all.

Boarding over the under-frame to form a shelf is also questionable as to advantage. Too often this shelf becomes another surface to clean of shavings and sawdust. On the other hand it *can* form a useful storage space for tool boxes and equipment in the small shop, even though it hides from sight tools and other objects that fall on the floor and roll under the bench.

Vise. The principal bench attachment is the vise. This is of the parallel-jaw type, made of metal but having the jaws faced with hard wood, preferably maple. The method of attachment depends upon the design, but it should be as close to the left-hand end of the bench as possible. The top of the jaws should be level with the bench top.

It is quite possible to do with one vise to a bench, but in handling long pieces of wood, a second vise at the other end is often a distinct advantage. The whole stick can be held rigidly, and the entire edge planed without moving the board once it is placed in position. It is even more helpful on a longer bench such as many shops use. On occasion it is also useful in permitting two men to work at the bench at the same time, and it is always a boon to the left-handed man.

Bench Stops. Bench stops are solid projections against which the work is held on the bench top. These can be of either wood or metal, adjustable or fixed. The adjustable types, which can be raised or lowered to suit the work, obviously are the most useful, and the metal designs have some advantages over the wooden ones.

The simplest stop is a square wooden (oak or

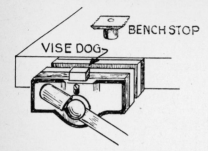

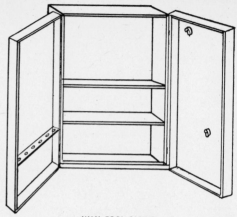

WALL TOOL CABINET

maple) peg let in a hole in the bench top. The peg is tapered or notched so that it won't fall through. A refinement is to have the peg stepped at different levels on two sides so that it can be set in the hole at different heights.

The metal stops also can be had in the fixed or adjustable forms. The most useful of all is probably the sliding metal stop which can be raised or lowered to any desired height by merely pulling it up or pushing it down. The top is a flat square of metal with fine teeth at one end and coarse teeth at the other so that it will hold all kinds of wood—hard or soft, rough or smooth—according to which way the teeth are turned. The danger with the metal stop is that you may set it too high while planing and forget to lower it till the plane strikes it and ruins the edge of the iron.

It is often an advantage to have two stops side by side, three or four inches apart, at the left-hand end of the bench. Then you can plane wide boards without moving them. At least one of the stops should be in line with the vise dog (the metal tongue in the middle of the vise jaw) so that you can use the vise to hold pieces too wide to go between its jaws.

Tool Rack. In most cases it is very convenient to have a tool rack mounted on the back board of the bench. Here you can keep the most-used tools for any particular job you are working on at the moment. Normally, perhaps, it would hold chisels,

screwdrivers, pliers, square, and hammer. For more permanent storage, shallow wall cupboards are usually best, leaving the bench as clear as possible. All of this, however, is largely a matter of personal preference, though it can be quite a nuisance having to leave the bench every time another tool is wanted. Tool cupboard design is discussed in detail later.

Bench Hook. A very useful adjunct to the bench is a bench hook. This is merely a flat board, about 6" x 12", with a block fastened to each end, one on top, one underneath. The upper one does not

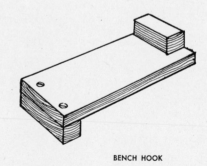

BENCH HOOK

extend the full width of the board at the right-hand end. The underside transverse piece rests against the front of the bench top when the hook is in use; the other forms a stop again which you can hold pieces to be sawed by hand. Being short, this upper piece allows you to saw through the work without marring the bench top.

Shooting Boards. Where a bench hook holds the work for sawing, shooting boards hold it for planing. They are particularly useful in working on the end grain, and can be arranged for straight or angle cuts.

A typical shooting board for angle planing consists of two pieces of wood cut to 45 degrees and screwed to a baseboard so that they form a right-angle space between them. Into this space is dropped a thick triangular piece that projects above the others. This triangular block forms a pair of cheeks against which the work can be held. The plane is laid on its side on the baseboard and slid along the angle so that it trims the work end at 45 degrees.

Another shooting board that enables you to plane the end grain of a board without splitting off a sliver at the end of the stroke is even more easily made. It is merely a baseboard about 8 inches wide and 20 inches long, with a 4-inch board screwed on top along one edge. This forms a right-angle groove along which the plane, laid on its side, can be slid. On one end of the top piece is a heavy block against which the work is held. This shooting board is intended to be held in the vise, but others will work equally well against the bench stops.

A somewhat similar device is the miter planing rig. This is really a clamp made from three trangular wood blocks and a thick base chamfered along one edge at 45 degrees. Two of the blocks are fixed, one at each end of the base. One of them forms the threaded holder for the clamping screw. The center block is arranged to slide along a groove in the base. Turning the screw clamps the work between the sliding block and the fixed end block.

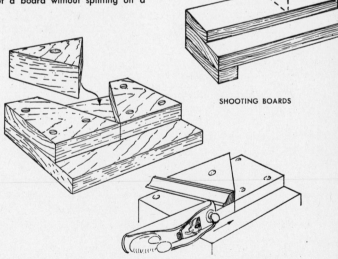

SHOOTING BOARDS

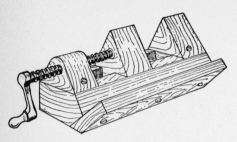

MITER PLANING RIG

Since the faces of all three blocks are lined up to form a 45-degree slope, it is easy to run the plane along them and so trim the work which has been rough-sawed to the same slope.

Other varieties of shooting boards can be devised for special jobs as they arise.

Tool and Supply Storage. Hanging things on the end of the bench is not recommended. They clatter, fall off, and collect dust, and look generally untidy. It is far better to put the smaller items in wall cabinets as near the eye level as possible. Such cabinets should be made shallow (3 to 5 inches, according to the size of the tools it is to contain) so that one item does not block access to another. You do not want to snag your hand on drill points while reaching for the brace. Nothing should be put in front of anything else. Large objects such as long clamps can be hung on the wall, preferably under a cabinet which will protect them, in some degree, from dust.

Since cupboards hang on the wall, generally at least three feet from the floor, they should not be more than three feet tall. Then everything will be readily seen and easily reached. Keeping things at or near eye level is especially important in connection with nails and screws. If you have packages of screws these are best stored in rows, and stacked not more than two high. The same thing applies to brads and finishing nails that come in boxes.

Hand Tools

Special tools required will depend almost entirely on the type of work you intend to do, but there is a long list of basic tools needed in almost every shop whether you have a power saw or not. Here is a list of the hand tools that should enable you to perform most of the operations called for in ordinary cabinet work:

Saws:

Crosscut saw, 26-inch, 11 points per inch (10 teeth).
Rip saw, 24-inch, 8 points to the inch (7 teeth).
Back saw, 12-inch, 13 points to the inch (12 teeth).
Dovetail saw, 10-inch, 15 points per inch, round handle.
Miter box saw, 22 inches long 11 points.
Compass saw, 14-inch, 10 points.
Keyhole saw, 10-inch, 10 points.
Coping saw, 6½-inch, 17-point blades.
Hack saw with 24 teeth per inch blades.

Planes:

Block plane, 6-inch.
Smoothing or bench plane, 8-inch.
Jack plane, 14-inch.
Rabbet plane or combination plane.

Drills:

Rachet brace.
Auger bits: ¼, ⅜, ½, ⅝, ¾, ⅞, 1-inch.
Countersink bit.
Forstner bits: ¼, ⅜, ½-inch.
Hand drill.
Twist drills: Nos. 1 to 60 wire gauge; drill points: ¹⁄₁₆, ⁵⁄₆₄, ³⁄₃₂, ⁷⁄₆₄, ⅛, ⁹⁄₆₄, ⁵⁄₃₂, ¹¹⁄₆₄.
Expansive bits: ¾-to-1½ inches, 1½-to-3½ inches.

Screwdrivers:

Cabinets: ⁵⁄₁₆ x 9 inches, ¼ x 7 inches, ⅛ x 6 inches, ¼-inch stubby.
Screwdriver bits for use with brace: ⁵⁄₁₆ and ³⁄₁₆.

Chisels:

Firmers, bevel edged: ¼, ⅜, ½, ¾, and 1-inch.
Mortise chisels: ¼ and ½-inch.
Cold chisel: ½-inch.
Gouges, ¼ and ½-inch.

Files:

Cabinet file, half-round, 8-inch.
Fine-cut, half-round.
Smooth mill file, 8-inch.
Taper saw file.
Crosscut saw file.

Pliers:

Diagonals.
Pincers.
Side-cutters.
Adjustable wrench, 8-inch.

Hammers:

Claw hammer, 12-oz.
Tack hammer.
Ball-pene (machinist's) hammer.
Mallet (wooden or plastic soft-faced).

Clamps:

2 Jorgensen adjustable steel-spindle hand screws, 8-inch (open to 4½ inches).
2 Jorgensen adjustable steel-spindle hand screws, 12-inch (open to 8½ inches).
2 sets bar clamp fittings for use on ¾-inch pipe.
2 bar clamps, 4 feet.
1 Jorgensen miter clamp.
Several small C- and spring clamps.

Miscellaneous:

Mitre box (preferably metal).
Nail sets: ¹⁄₁₆, ³⁄₃₂-inch.
Bench brush.
Brad awl.
Scratch awl or sharp-pointed knife.
Saw set (saw filing vise).
Spokeshave, 10-inch (2⅛-inch cutter).
Open-throat router, 3 cutters.
Butt gauge.
Bit gauge.
Marking gauge (or combined marking and mortise).
Steel square, 24-inch.
Try square (or try and miter square), 8-inch blade.
Combination square, 12-inch.
Bevel, sliding T, 8-inch blade.
Level, 12-inch, wood.
Dividers.
Steel rule, 12-inch.
Dowel sharpener.
Doweling jig (usable as bit guide in mortising).
Steel (or boxwood) rule, 6-foot, folding.

Very few beginners will want to get all this equipment at once, and some who confine their activities to a small variety of pieces will not need all items. It may be advisable to decide first on the one piece he will build as a starter, and buy only the tools necessary to make that piece. From then on more tools may be added as they are required and found essential. Too often it happens that the enthusiastic novice buys several tools that he uses rarely or not at all, so it is best to proceed slowly in the beginning. In any case the best procedure usually is to get only the essentials at first, such as crosscut saw, hammer, screwdriver, chisel, etc., and add to them the other tools as the need for each of them arises. If this can be done without inconvenience, the acquisition of a complete outfit over a period of time is practically painless.

Tool Sharpening. The four principal types of cutting tools that will need to be kept sharp are: chisels, planes, saws, and drills. Chisels include gouges, while planes include the spokeshave and router. Both chisels and plane irons are sharpened in the same manner. If the sharp edge of any of these tools is nicked or blunted it will need grinding. For this purpose you need a grinding wheel of aluminum oxide, either hand or motor driven. With the hand-operated type it is necessary to have someone turn while you hold the tool. A motor-driven grinder, preferably with two wheels (a rough and a smooth) is therefore a good investment. The plane, chisel, and spokeshave blades are all ground to about 25 degrees. In using the high-speed wheel, care needs to be taken to see that the blade doesn't become so hot as to lose temper. If it gets red hot at the tip, then turns blue, it will be soft and need re-tempering. With care, this need not happen, but in any case you should have a can of water handy for dipping the tool into after each short pass across the wheel. After a rough cut, the blade can be given a short finish grind on the smooth wheel.

In grinding see that the end of the blade is kept square to the wheel, and check its squareness before and after grinding. The next step is to hone the blade by rubbing the ground bevel on an oil-stone. Apply a little oil to the rough side of the oil-stone, and, holding the blade so that the bevel lies flat on the stone, rub it back and forth in a figure-eight motion. To remove the feather edge that forms in grinding and sharpening, turn the blade over, lay it flat on the stone and rub it back and forth a couple of times. Finish sharpening on the fine side of the stone. If a leather hone is available so much the better.

Sharpening a gouge is a little more difficult because of the curved blade. Some gouges are beveled on the inside and some on the outside, and the procedure differs accordingly. Those with an outside bevel are ground on the wheel in the same manner as a chisel, but the point is turned slowly, first one way then the other, till the whole curved surface is equally ground. Some find this easier to do on the side of the wheel instead of the edge.

In the case of inside bevels you have either to use a special thin wheel with a rounded rim, or do it by hand with a round-edged slip stone. After grinding, the outside bevel can be whetted on an oilstone in the same manner as a chisel except that the gouge must be rolled as it is rubbed. The inside gouge is whetted with a very fine slip stone.

Auger bits are sharpened by hand with a special file. This file has two flat, tapered ends, one with teeth on the sides, the other toothed on the edges. The toothed sides are used for sharpening the nibs and the edges are used to sharpen the lips. No honing is needed.

The sharpening of saws is a much more complicated procedure than any of the foregoing. The process, which is called "fitting," consists of three operations: jointing, setting, and filing. In jointing, all the teeth are made the same length; setting is the bendng of the teeth sideways to the proper angle, and filing sharpens the teeth. In attempting this job of saw fitting the amateur should procure a saw vise that is equipped with a file guide.

The length of the teeth is equalized by running a file or stone along the edges of the teeth. It simplifies matters if you set the file halfway into a strip of wood of the same length before using it on the teeth. It will then run straight and not slide off to snag your fingers. The saw is then ready for setting.

The first step now is to secure the saw in the vise with about half the blade above the jaws. This allows room to manipulate the setting tool. This tool aptly is called a saw set. It looks like a heavy pair of pliers, but one jaw contains a heavy steel disc or anvil; the other an adjustable screw. The anvil can be revolved to regulate the angle it makes with the screw, and this controls the degree to which the saw tooth is bent over.

Put the "set" over one saw tooth at a time so that the screw presses against the tooth tip. When you squeeze the handles, the screw bends the tooth against the anvil. After each alternate tooth has been bent in this manner, the saw is turned around in the vise and the rest of the teeth are bent in the opposite direction. The saw is then ready for filing.

The type of file used depends on the type of saw. For a crosscut saw the teeth are made to form a series of sharp points, beveled toward the inside. For that reason they are filed at an angle of 45 degrees.

The rip saw, however, has teeth that form a series of tiny flat-edged chisels. This necessitates filing them straight across at 90 degrees. As before, the alternate teeth are filed, then the saw is reversed and the intermediate teeth are filed.

For the rip saw the file is triangular to fit in between the teeth. For the crosscut a thinner file is used, but it cuts an edge on two teeth at a time. After the filing is finished, any burrs on the sides of the teeth may be removed by laying the saw flat and running an oil stone lightly over them.

Holding Devices

In much of the hand work done upon the wood, both before and after assembly, it is necessary to have it held rigidly. The bench vise and stops are not always sufficient for this and other arrangements are necessary.

Sometimes a notched board on the bench will hold an odd-shaped piece, but more generally we need holding tools such as portable vises, hand screws, clamps, and clamping jigs.

There is a large variety of bar clamps available, from the flat steel kind to the gaspipe variety. The latter consist of a sliding jaw and a crank jaw that fit over any piece of ¾-inch iron pipe that is threaded at one end. With this arrangement you can make a clamp of any length at all, provided you have the necessary piece of pipe. Another type of bar clamp uses a wood bar, and this has the advantage of being less likely to mar the work

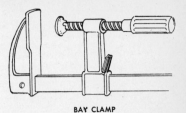

BAY CLAMP

than the metal kind. The T-bar steel clamp is made as a unit in lengths up to 4 feet or more.

The C-clamps with which you can hold work to the bench top, to a board, or any two parts together, are available in many sizes from three inches up. The most useful sizes for cabinet shop use are the 4-inch and 8-inch sizes.

Finally, there are the hand screws that will hold pieces of either regular or irregular shape. The

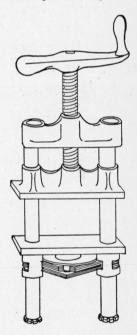

TWIN BAR CLAMP

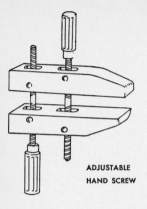

ADJUSTABLE
HAND SCREW

Saw Horses and Saw Bench

In sawing long pieces of stock and trimming, or otherwise working upon large flat assemblies such as table tops, it is an advantage to be able to lay the material flat. This is best done by using a pair of trestles or saw horses. The horses are very easily knocked together from five piece of 2" x 4", one

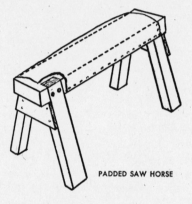

PADDED SAW HORSE

most versatile of these are the style known as adjustable because the jaws can be set at almost any angle to one another. In the non-adjustable type the jaws do remain parallel, and these also have their uses. Both kinds consist of a pair of wooden jaws mounted on two screwed steel spindles. Each spindle has a right-handed thread for half its length and a left-handed thread along the other half. Turning either spindle therefore causes both jaws to move in relation to it. To adjust the clamp quickly you hold both handles and revolve the whole clamp by rotating the handles around one another. This causes both jaws to open, or close, depending on the direction the handles are turning.

On occasion, when there are not sufficient clamps available, it may be necessary to devise other means of holding assemblies together. If the work is flat it may be possible to lay it on a flat surface and apply pressure by wedging it inside a frame, or between two heavy battens. In the case of chairs and other odd-shaped pieces, the simplest solution may be a rope tourniquet—a light but strong rope tightened around the structure and pulled taut by twisting a heavy stick through a loop in the line. Ingenuity will always find a way.

forming the top and four the legs. They are best fastened together by bolts.

To protect cabinet woods from dents it pays to cover the tops of the horses with heavy cloth, rubber, or a strip of baize or felt. The standard height of the trestles is 22 inches, but make them to suit your own leg length—the knee often forms an

SAWING BENCH

efficient steady-rest. The legs need to be splayed sideways so that the horse will not rock or tip over endwise.

Even more useful than the horses on occasion is a sawing bench. This is merely a heavy table, the same height as the trestles or a little lower. The top should be of heavy plank, and the legs vertical, not splayed. The top needs to be about 12" x 30" allowing a 1½-inch overhang all around for clamping the work. This, too, should have a padded top to avoid scarring finished surfaces. If you can contrive a removable pad, so much the better.

Power Tools

Nearly all operations called for in ordinary cabinet making can be performed with the hand tools discussed on the preceding pages. Wood can be obtained from some yards and mills, planed, cut to size, as well as turnings and other parts for assembling and finishing.

Therefore power tools should be considered only after a realistic appraisal of the intended extent of your operations.

There are so many types and varieties of woodworking machines available for the smaller shop that it is often difficult to know which to install first. A complication arises from the fact that certain tools can be had in combination with others, thus offering possibilities for savings in both cost and floor space. Some of these combination tools work out quite well in a one-man shop, but those that require a great deal of adjustment in changing over from one kind of an operation to another are not so acceptable. The drawback to many of these tools is that only one unit can be used at a time, and if the operator acquires a helper, temporary or permanent, time will be lost through the whole machine being tied up for one operation. As a rule, therefore, in a shop where serious work is to be done and expansion is anticipated separate machine tools are preferable to combinations, provided space permits. And each tool should have its own motor.

Under the head of power tools come both the stationary and portable units. The stationary ones include the circular or bench saw, band saw, jig saw, bench sander, drill, jointer-planer, shaper, and the lathe. A tool grinder is also a practical necessity for sharpening chisels, plane irons, and other tools. The portable units consist of electric saws and drills, the latter having attachments for driving screws, and special sanding and buffing operations.

Circular Saw. Almost always the first thing that should be acquired by the serious cabinet maker is a circular saw, probably with a dado attachment for cutting grooves. With a combination blade the saw will cut either along or across the grain. An 8-inch blade will cut wood up to 2⅜ inches thick, and the 10-inch blade will cut up to 3⅜ inches.

With such a saw you can cut your stock to any length or thickness, cut miters at any angle, make rabbets and grooves (both square and round, and bevels).

All modern circular saws have the blade mounted on an arbor that can be screwed up or down to regulate the height of the blade above the table. The simpler and less expensive type also allows the table to be tilted to 45 degrees to one side. Working on this tilted surface complicates the use of the saw and also introduces an element of danger to the operator. It therefore pays to acquire a better and somewhat more expensive professional type of saw in which the blade itself tilts and the table remains horizontal.

The most important attachment for the circular saw is a dado head. This cuts a flat-bottomed groove either with or across the grain. The head consists of a pair of outside cutters having both crosscut and rip teeth. Clamped between them are one or more double-ended cutters that space them the required distance apart and serve to remove the chips. Such cutter assemblies will cut grooves with the grain or dadoes across it from ⅛ to ¹³⁄₁₆ inch on some 8-inch saws, and up to 2 inches on some 10-inch saws.

Band Saws. The two types of saws that cut irregular shapes are the band saw and the jig saw. The principal difference between them is that the band saw has a continuous ribbon-type blade driven in one direction only—downward through the work. The jig saw, on the other hand, has a much finer blade that "jigs" up and down, its actual length of travel being only an inch or so. The band saw, having a heavy blade and running in one direction only, is a much more powerful tool than the jig saw, and will cut through much thicker and harder wood. Such a tool is practically essential where curves are to be cut in heavy stock, and very deep cuts made edgewise through boards. The same cut-out work can be done on a number of thin pieces stacked and temporarily fastened together. Curved chair back and legs are simple to make with a band saw. The blades ordinarily used will be ⅛, ¼, and ⅜ widths, though the larger tools will take a ½-inch blade with ease.

With the narrowest blade you can make curves and circles to about a 3-inch radius (6-inch circle), but the size of work the saw handles will be limited by the size of the piece of wood you are working on. The distance between the blade and the supporting arm of a 14-inch band saw is generally about 13⅜ inches—sufficient for most jobs in the smaller shop.

If you get a standard 12- or 14-inch saw you may also be able to fit it with an extension block that will increase the space between the table and the upper guide by an additional 6 inches or so. This is useful in sawing odd-shaped pieces or those partly assembled. But do not attempt to cut through very thick stock that will buckle the blade, overheat, and probably snap it.

Jig Saw. The jig saw is used almost exclusively for cutting out simple or intricate patterns in thin stock. The professional types of jig saws will handle the saber-type blade as well as the usual jig saw blade. The saber-type is held only at one end and therefore does not need to be uncoupled in removing the work. Modern saws also incorporate a small piston to blow the sawdust away from the work, and a lamp to illuminate the working area. Most generally useful are the jig saws that have a tilting table and a variable speed adjustment. For maximum utility, a saw with at least 20 inches clearance between the saw and its supporting arm should be procured. A 24-inch tool will not be too big.

Sander. Bench sanders are available in a variety of types and sizes, but in a small shop where there is very little repetition work a medium-sized, general-purpose unit is best. This should have a flat table under the belt and a roller at each end, and be adjustable for either vertical or horizontal work. The belt need be no more than 4½ inches wide and about 27 inches long. Flat surfaces are sanded on the table and can be held against a fence across the belt which is adjustable to various angles. The flat part of the belt is used for level surfaces and the sections between the plate ends and the rollers and over the rollers themselves are used for inside and outside curves. This type of sander usually has a sanding disc, 9 inches or more in diameter, mounted on one of the roller shafts. This has its own adjustable table and miter gauge, and is invaluable in trimming ends square or to an angle.

If a great number of long pieces such as chair legs have to be sanded, a different type of belt sander, having a long, flexible belt, may have advantages, but the ordinary shop will get adequate service from the bench sander described and three or four grades of belts, from fine to coarse grit.

Drill Press. A bench drill or floor-type drill press can be a great time-saver both as a drill and as a router for carving, recessing, and making dovetail joints. Boring and countersinking are common operations, and a very simple attachment turns the drill bit into a mortise cutter. This tool is merely a hollow square chisel or cutter that fits around the drill. As the drill makes its circular hole the cutter trims the hole square.

A drill press to perform all these operations, plus internal sanding, needs to operate at a fairly wide range of speeds. For most purposes, in the small shop, a tool that will take up to a half-inch drill bit should be adequate. Since large pieces may have to be handled, a floor-type drill is best because the table can be lowered three feet or more below the drill chuck.

Jointer. This high-speed cutting tool makes board edges perfectly smooth and straight for jointing. It also planes surfaces up to 4 inches or 6 inches wide according to the size of the tool, and is used for tapering, rabbeting and beveling, and planing both sides of a board parallel. Extreme care is necessary in using this tool because the cutting head, which revolves at high speed, is often exposed and, since the boards are narrow, the operator's hands of necessity come close to it.

The jointer may be of either bench or floor type, and the smallest practical size is the 4-inch model. This is large enough for the small shop as a rule.

The tool consists of a front and rear table with a cutting head between their adjacent ends. The work is done by sliding the wood from the rear to the front tables over the cutter. The manner in which the cutter trims the wood depends on the relative positions of the two tables and the cutting head. For example, if the front table is ⅛ inch lower than the rear table, and the rear table level with the cutters, a cut ⅛ inch deep will be taken off the length of the board. Raising the rear table above the cutter could take a taper cut off the work, and so on. This tapering, however, should not be attempted by anyone not thoroughly familiar

with the machine, and only then when extreme care is taken—fingers can too easily be lost.

Shaper. Another useful machine with which it does not pay to take liberties is the shaper. This tool has a vertical spindle on which can be mounted a variety of toothed cutters that are made to revolve at extremely high speeds. Cutters of various shapes are used to make grooves, mouldings, fluting, and beads. For the advanced worker on the more elaborate furniture pieces the shaper is a great timesaver, but it is rarely a necessity in the small shop where a hand-operated shaper is more likely to fill the occasional need.

The Lathe. Turnings enter into a great many pieces of furniture, both classical and modern, not only for chairs and tables but for brackets and decorative parts of cabinets, beds, and other larger pieces. In the fully-equipped shop, a lathe is practically essential. For all normal purposes, a four-speed, 12-inch, ball-bearing lathe, to take a piece 37 inches between centers should be sufficient. Longer pieces can often be built up in several sections joined by dowels or turned shanks. The foregoing figures mean that a piece up to 12-inch diameter and 37 inches long can be worked on. The four speeds, probably 900, 1,400, 2,200, and 3,400 r.p.m., will be sufficient for practically all work on wood, including large face-plate turning.

This type of lathe is best driven through a V belt by a motor solidly attached to the base. There is, however, no objection to the bench lathe provided both it and the motor are rigidly mounted in relation to one another. In all cases there should be a quickly accessible switch in case of accidents.

With such a lathe and a complete set of turning tools—and of course the skill to use them—you can make all kinds of spindles, legs, rails, split turnings, threads, and so forth. Then, with a number of simple jigs and attachments you can do special sanding, wire brushing, buffing, grinding, boring, and make dowels and do fluting and reeding. The lathe also saves time in finishing turned parts. Various finishes can be applied—wax, oil, varnish, shellac, french polish—with the work revolving at slow speeds between centers or on the outboard face plate. The standard set of turning chisels consists of the following: ¼-inch gouge; ½-inch skew, spear; ½-inch gouge, parting tool, round-nose; ¾-inch gouge; 1-inch skew.

There are two methods of turning—one by cutting or paring, the other by scraping. The scraping method is much the simpler and is quite often indulged in by beginners in learning to use the lathe. Experts disagree as to which gives the best results in competent hands. Theoretically, the cutting method should be quicker and cleaner, but the fact remains that many competent wood turners use the scraping method and rely on sanding to finish the work smooth. One advantage of scraping, it is claimed, is that there is much less chance of a chisel slipping and spoiling the work. This alone might well recommend scraping to beginners. The ideal system, however, would be for the beginner to familiarize himself with both methods and make a final decision only when he is skilled in handling the tools. By that time his aptitude with one method or the other will doubtless have settled the problem for him.

As the above may suggest, the art of turning is something that cannot be learned from text books. The only satisfactory way is to do the work under the watchful eye of a competent worker, and learn from your mistakes. It can be pointed out, however, that in making turnings observation of a couple of simple rules will make all the difference between a nice-appearing job and a clumsy one.

On many turnings there are combinations of

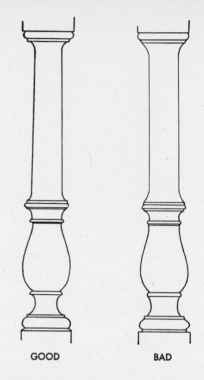

GOOD   BAD

shoulders with recesses or rounds (coves or beads), as you see in the illustration. Strange as it may seem, if the shoulder is not exactly square (i.e., parallel with the center line of the turning) and the curves do not meet the shoulder at right angles, the turning will have an unattractive look.

Even where two curves come together they should flow into one another and not meet at an angle. Careful attention to these details will make the difference between an excellent and a mediocre turning; between good design and poor execution.

CIRCULAR SAW

LATHE

JOINTER

DRILL PRESS

BAND SAW

SHAPER

JIG SAW

HOME WORKSHOP POWER TOOLS

Woods, Accessories, Supplies

Chapter III

WATERLOO HIGH SCHOOL LIBRARY
1464 INDUSTRY RD.
ATWATER, OHIO 44201

Woods, Accessories, Supplies

Hard Woods and Soft Woods

Before discussing the different kinds of wood, it is necessary to clear up a common point of confusion that arises from the arbitrary classification of woods by the lumber trade.

In the lumber business all woods that come from conifers, i.e., trees that have needles or scale-like leaves, are classed as softwoods, and all woods from broadleaved trees are called hardwoods. Note that in this connection both softwood and hardwood are spelled as one word.

Unfortunately for a clear understanding, not all the softwoods are soft in character, nor are all the so-called hardwoods hard. To avoid confusion, therefore, in this text, we shall refer to all woods that are soft as soft woods (two words)—which means that they are less fibrous and more easy to cut than the hard woods, as well as being lighter in weight. The other woods we shall call hard woods (two words) because they actually are hard, their texture being dense, which makes them heavy and tough.

With this distinction made clear, we can set the matter aside for the moment while we look into the actual differences between the so-called hardwoods and softwoods. An understanding of these things is often of help in identifying woods and cataloging their working characteristics. Once you understand the difference in structure between the two kinds of wood you can usually, with the aid of

24

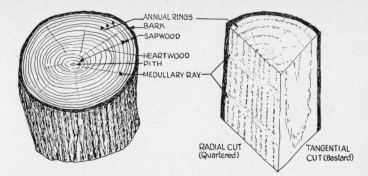

RADIAL CUT
(Quartered)

TANGENTIAL
CUT (Bastard)

a magnifying glass, tell whether the specimen you are studying is a hardwood or a softwood in the lumberman's language.

All natural wood, then, is made up of cells. In the soft woods these cells are all of the kind that are very small and closed at both ends. These tough little sealed tubes are called fibers. Similar cells are also found in most of the hardwoods, but, in addition there will be many large, open-ended cells or pores. In some woods these large pores can be seen without the aid of a lens, but in any case they are one reason why some hardwoods need fillers before painting or varnishing.

In both the hardwoods and softwoods there are also short, flat cells radiating outward from the center of the tree toward the bark. These form what are called medullary rays, and in some kinds of wood they are much more prominent than in others. Their significance will be apparent when we have looked into the matter of cutting the tree trunk into planks and boards.

Sawing Systems

There are several ways of cutting a tree trunk into usable lumber. The simplest is to saw the log lengthwise the full width of the trunk. The taper and varying thicknesses of the trunk give the flat-sawn boards the typical V-shaped surface grain.

The log can also be cut diagonally, that is, across the grain at right angles to the annular rings. The grain then appears as straight lines along the face of the board. If the saw has cut through any of the medullary rays mentioned above, there will be flaky streaks across the grain. Quite often these flakes give the grain an attractive appearance that it otherwise would not have had. The flakes are usually not so strongly marked in softwoods, and the radial surface is called vertical or edge grain.

Apart from the grain figure, the advantage of using edge-grain or quarter-sawed boards is that they do not warp so much in seasoning as the plain-sawed boards, nor shrink and expand excessively with changes in atmospheric moisture.

All wood is seasoned and dried after cutting. This may be done by leaving the boards exposed to the air in a dry shed for a considerable period of time. In the old days one or two years was considered the minimum, but nowadays we are satisfied with a few months and the lumber quality suffers as a consequence.

Another method is to dry the wood more rapidly in special kilns. This usually reduces the moisture content below what it normally will be when the wood is in use. Therefore the wood must be allowed to pick up some moisture from the air before it is checked for warping and bending. All things considered, then, the beginner in woodworking should deal with a lumber yard or supply house of good reputation while learning to judge the qualities of cabinet woods himself.

Wood Selection

The identification and selection of woods for use in the cabinet shop is not a subject that can easily be learned from books. Colored illustrations would help, but you need to become acquainted with woods by actually handling them, and having someone, expert on the subject, identify them for you. Frequent visits to the furniture-wood dealers is a great help in this respect because you can see the different varieties side by side and know exactly what you are looking at. Here we shall have to be content with brief descriptions.

It does help to have on hand a reliable book on woods for reference, or even a dealer's illustrated catalog. One reason is that many of the furniture woods have several names and even local appellations. There are about fifty kinds of wood called mahogany, and even four or five known as whitewood. An outstanding example of confused nomenclature is Douglas fir which is known as Oregon pine and is neither fir nor pine but a species all its own.

In spite of these deterrents it is surprisingly easy to know woods when you have handled them for a short time, and as for the rest there is little point in being scientifically correct so long as the wood you use for a particular job works well and looks as good as it should.

In many, if not most, pieces of furniture, a variety of woods is used. For example, a walnut piece might have drawer sides, back, and bottom of poplar, and drawer slides and other hidden parts of pine. Such things are recognized good practice and that does not necessarily cheapen a piece in any way. This is particularly true in the case of pieces made to be painted. The important factors here are design, resistance to damage and wear, and the ability to take and hold the finish.

The Furniture Woods

The principal woods used in furniture making are poplar, basswood, pine, maple, oak, birch, cherry, beech, walnut, gumwood, mahogany, apple, and pear.

Other woods such as elm, beech, sycamore, and ash are used principally for concealed parts such as the frames of upholstered pieces where appearance does not matter but strength does. Less often used are butternut (sometimes called white walnut) and white cedar, while hickory, ash, and birch made spindles and small bent parts, the birch also being used for legs.

In furniture making the choice of wood depends upon a number of things such as strength, hardness, and resistance to damage that is required as well as the color and decorative markings. For painted pieces the plainer woods like poplar and pine may well be used.

Poplar. Poplar, though tinged with pale green, also is called whitewood. Like basswood (also sometimes called whitewood or, more properly, linden) it is cheap, and easy to finish but has little grain and therefore no character. The poplar is quite brittle and subject to warping. For these reasons its use is largely confined to places where it does not show, such as drawer sides and backs. It is also used for cheap furniture parts such a table tops that are to be painted, and as a base for veneers. When used in large areas it is usually cut into fairly narrow strips and re-joined with the grain alternating in direction, thus minimizing warping. Basswood is a little scarcer than poplar, otherwise one can be substituted for the other without gain or loss.

Pine. There are two kinds of pine commonly used in furniture—the white and the yellow varieties. White pine has a straight and even grain and a pleasing texture, and finishes well. It is light in weight, and the sapwood is white, with the heart-wood ranging from pinkish white to gray.

Though quite soft and easily dented, white pine does make attractive provincial furniture, especially when antiqued. It is used largely for small pieces and accessories such as hanging shelves and cupboards, and kitchen furniture such as Welsh dressers, corner cupboards, and so forth.

The yellow or short-leaf variety of pine is not a good cabinet wood. Like fir it has a very pronounced grain that makes it difficult to finish to a very smooth surface. If it is used at all the sapwood is to be preferred, and it should be fairly free from knots. The so-called knotty pine is colorful and has its uses, but it should not be used for large areas. A knot here and there helps, but a rash of them spoils any piece. Such wood is best painted, as it was in the old days.

White Cedar. Another soft wood that is delightful to work with and lovely to look at is white cedar. It has a beautiful grain and delicate shadings of color, but it should not be used in large masses. A cupboard entirely of white cedar with a transparent finish would be rather overpowering, but such a piece in pine with cedar panels could be most attractive.

Maple. Maple is of course a perennial favorite, both for painted and unpainted pieces whether of modern or traditional design. Some striking effects can be secured by using the modern transparent finishes.

Maple comes in a variety of colors from off-white to light brown, and with wavy, curly, or birdseye grain markings. Because of its hardness it can be given a sharp edge, and makes turnings with thin edges that do not break off as pine does. The hard sugar maple is the variety most commonly used.

Oak. Oak is another furniture wood with a marked grain that is often variegated and quite ornamental. Both the white and red oaks are much used, the principal difference being deeper red-brown color of the red oak heartwood. The white oak is more durable and less porous than the red and seems to finish better.

Being somewhat hard and brittle, especially when old, oak is not as easy to work as pine, but it lends itself very well to carving. It can be left its natural color, bleached, filled with a white filler, or darkened to a very rich antique-looking tone.

Old oak often becomes very brittle and joints need to be made of ample size if they are to be subjected to bending or twisting stresses.

Birch. Birch may be the wood of either the yellow or the sweet birch. The heartwood of both is called red birch and the sapwood white birch, and when dark stains are applied the difference cannot be detected.

This wood is somewhat tougher than oak but rather easier to work on account of its smooth grain. It has a light tone and takes a high polish. Consequently it is particularly adapted to modern sleek styles of furniture and as a substitute for maple. Because it shrinks considerably in drying it should be well seasoned before using.

Cherry. Cherry is a close-grained wood, somewhat softer than beech or birch, and of a warm brown color. It looks something like a pale mahogany, but there is little figure in the grain, except in the burls. It takes a high polish and is a nice wood to work with and, although relatively scarce, is often used in making antique reproductions.

Beech. Both red beech and white beech are from the same tree, one being the heartwood and the other the sapwood. Both woods are fairly hard with a fine, straight grain, though liable to warp and check. The non-distinctive character of the grain, and its ability to take stains well, make beech a popular substitute for other woods such as mahogany, rosewood, or even ebony. It is popular for turnings and is often used for French Provincial pieces, stained to a fruitwood such as apple.

Walnut. The commonest walnut used for furniture in this country is the black variety which comes in various shades of color from chocolate to light brown. Long a favorite for fine cabinet work, it can be turned or carved, and finishes beautifully.

Much more fancy is the Circassian walnut which is streaked with black and dark brown. In both kinds the burls and crotches are extremely decorative.

Gumwood. One of the most versatile of all furniture woods is gumwood, particularly in the low-priced field. It can be stained and finished to look like mahogany, walnut, maple, and even oak.

Gumwood is also used as a veneer, as well as in the solid, and in either form it is much less expensive than any of the woods it imitates, but it needs to be finished with care or it will look as cheap as it is.

In its natural state, gum heartwood may be any color from a pale pink to a rich reddish brown. In making furniture for yourself it is usually much more satisfying to work in the genuine wood than in any imitation or substitute. However, the rarer figured red gum makes beautiful panels.

Mahogany. True mahogany is one of the aristocrats among furniture woods, and consequently has many imitators. It is not only pleasingly marked but rich in color and is readily worked and carved. Furthermore, it shrinks very little and is not inclined to split easily. Various types of interesting grain can be secured in quarter-sawed boards such as striped, curly, ribbon, mottle, crotch, fiddle-back, etc., and the wood is priced accordingly.

Whether used solid or as a veneer, mahogany has an inherent dignity so that it does not lend itself well to cheap pieces and kitchen furniture. The wood known as Philippine mahogany or lauan is a different wood entirely and has little to recommend it.

Sources of Wood Supply

In most large cities there are dealers in furniture woods, and practically all of the larger firms have illustrated catalogs. Many advertise in woodworking and crafts magazines and cater to mail-order business. Some sell mostly by mail, but as a rule it is best to pick out your pieces yourself. The commoner woods such as pine, poplar, and maple, can often be obtained from the local lumber yard, but care needs to be taken to see that these woods are properly seasoned. For one thing they should look, and feel, quite dry.

An oftimes useful source of good dry lumber is old furniture. This wood is especially valuable in making reproductions of antique pieces or any furniture in the traditional styles—Queen Anne, Chippendale, Sheraton, Hepplewhite, Phyfe, French Provincial, or even Early American. All such wood, however, needs to be closely examined for nails and other hardware fragments that may injure your tools, and for unapparent glue-joints. Also it is well to clean the surfaces of dirt and dust that make a damaging abrasive when sharp chisel, plane, and saw edges come in contact with it.

Plywood

In making modern furniture and built-in pieces, plywood can often be used with advantage. It gives wide surfaces without joints, and is extremely strong for its weight. Plywood is also used for non-structural parts such as drawer bottoms, partitions, and dust panels, and the backs of case pieces.

Although plywood has been used in furniture construction for many years, it is not often found on old

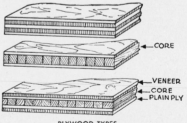

PLYWOOD TYPES

pieces of handmade furniture. For present-day pieces, however, it can often be employed with advantage, and in many built-in units it is practically indispensable. This is particularly true with regard to some of the modern types of plywood faced with the better furniture woods.

Plywood is nothing more than several layers of thin wood glued together under heat and high pressure. The strength of the sheet is greatly increased by arranging each layer so that the grain runs at right angles to that of the layers on either side of it. Sometimes the layers are of the same wood and of equal thickness. In other instances there is a thick core, with several thin layers on either side.

To avoid warping, the core wood is often cut into narrow strips, glued together with the grains running in opposite directions, end for end. Poplar is often used for this purpose, being light and cheap. In practically all plywoods the inside layers are made of lighter and cheaper woods than the outside ones so that both cost and weight are reduced.

The principal drawback to the use of ordinary plywoods for the visible surfaces of furniture is the grain. These plywood layers are made by rotating a log against a sharp knife. This cuts off a slice all round the log and so produces a grain pattern that cannot be disguised. This is the only way in which very wide and long sheets of thin wood can be secured.

The alternative is to saw slices through the widest part of a thick tree trunk. But such slices are limited to a width of three or four feet. Therefore, if the plywood base is to be covered with a surface layer of sawn wood, either the width will be very limited or the necessity for matching the surface slices will make the cost considerably higher. Nevertheless, plywoods with a veneer of some good furniture wood are readily obtainable and should be used in place of the less desirable common plywoods.

Veneers

The application of a surface of good furniture wood to a solid base of cheaper, stronger, or less decorative wood is called veneering—the outer layer being the veneer. The process of veneering has been practiced for about 4,000 years and on some very good furniture. The use of veneers does not necessarily mean cheap construction.

Until the nineteenth century, when machines were invented to cut the veneer, it was comparatively thick.

Many old veneers of the eighteenth century or earlier, being sawn by hand, were an eighth of an inch thick, or more. Today, the machine-sliced veneers are often a twenty-fifth of an inch or less in thickness. On the other hand, the actual application of the veneer to the wood base cannot satisfactorily be done by hand, except in the case of small patches. It is a factory process calling for hot presses and special glues. Hand work is therefore limited to quite small areas and ordinary repair jobs.

Inlays

In both solid wood and veneer it is common practice to let in small pieces or strips of thin wood of contrasting color for decorative purposes. This is called inlaying. One form which uses larger pieces or patterns of wood (holly, tulip, satinwood, etc.), metal, ivory, mother-of-pearl, etc., is known as marquetry. Another form, using tortoise-shell and different colored metals is called boulle work (often wrongly spelled buhl).

None of these forms of inlaying is very difficult, but they do call for special skills outside the province of this book. They also call for great restraint on the part of the worker if the results are to be in good taste.

Later we shall discuss other and more common forms of decoration applicable to old and new styles of furniture.

Furniture Accessories

On the majority of furniture pieces in the modern or non-traditional style, the wooden drawer knobs and handles are of designs that are easily made in the shop. Some of the traditional styles of wooden knobs also can be made on the lathe. On the other hand, if turned knobs are required and you do not have a lathe, it may be preferable to buy the knobs ready-made. Bought in quantities of a dozen or more they can be quite cheap, but it you want to make distinctive furniture, it is best to make, and perhaps even design, your own knobs. Even on re-producion pieces you can add a little extra feel of handwork by making them yourself.

In dealing with traditional styles of furniture it is essential to use the authentic design of knob or pull, and often these will be of metal. In order to ensure accuracy, it is well to check with the catalog of makers, some of whom are listed in the Appendix. A few of the principal period styles of knobs and pulls are illustrated.

Other accessories include stock escutcheons, finials, drops, foot sockets, bedpost bolt covers, chest lifts, hinges, locks, bolts, cupboard and table catches, desk leaf quadrants, and so forth. Nothing looks sillier to the initiated than a French Provincial drawer pull on a Queen Anne chest, or an Empire glass knob on an early Chippendale piece. And of course none of these is suitable for modern furniture of any kind. This is why it pays to study period styles, including those of today; apparently insignificant details can make or mar the finished job.

Metal Fastenings

This brief survey of cabinet shop materials must include also nails, screws, and similar fastenings. Headed nails are seldom used in cabinet work, though you will need plenty of tenpenny common nails for attaching built-in pieces to the walls and similar carpentry jobs. Otherwise, finishing nails, brads, and escutcheon pins are used almost exclu-

sively where it is not convenient or necessary to use screws. Tacks and gimp pins are used in upholstering.

The nails and the brads (small editions of nails), are driven below the surface of the wood by means of a nail-set that has a point no larger than the heads. The tiny holes are then filled with a paste filler. Screws likewise are buried by counterboring or deep countersinking and subsequently covering the heads.

In attaching metal parts it may be necessary to use round-headed or oval-headed screws, but in the majority of cases the flat, countersunk head is used. Exposed screws should be made of or coated with some non-corrosible metal such as brass, nickel, or chromium, or have a black gunmetal finish that will not tarnish.

Brads are obtainable in pound boxes, and their sizes range from 3/16 to 1 inch. They are used mostly for attaching moldings, thin lips, galleries, and so on. The finishing nails are available in lengths from 1 to 3 inches, which is about the maximum length

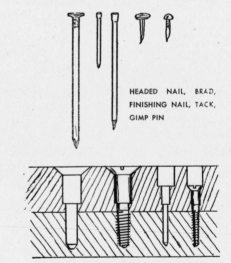

HEADED NAIL, BRAD,
FINISHING NAIL, TACK,
GIMP PIN

COUNTERSUNK AND COUNTERBORED SCREWS

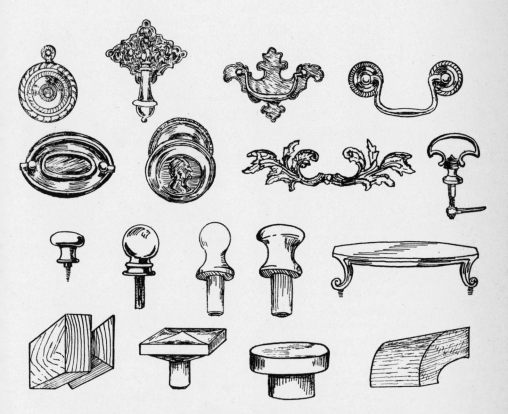

LEFT TO RIGHT: BEDPOST ROSETTE; TEAR DROP HANDLE; PLATE DRAWER PULL; BAIL HANDLE; OVAL
DRAWER PULL; BRASS KNOB; FRENCH TYPE PULL; CUPBOARD TURN; SCREW CUPBOARD KNOB;
CUPBOARD KNOB; 2 TAVERN KNOBS; CASH DRAWER PULL; MODERN WOODEN DRAWER KNOBS & PULLS

normally used in cabinet work. The brad sizes you will find the most use for seem to be the ½, ⅝, ¾, ⅞ and 1 inch. Brads also are sold in the 1¼ and 1½-inch sizes (all in 17 gauge) but at that point they really should be called finishing nails. The nails likewise run up to 3 inches by quarters in 18 gauge.

The assortment of screws kept on hand should include:

No. 5x½″	No. 3x⅞″	No. 8x1½″	No. 9x2″
8x½″	4x1″	9x1½″	10x2″
4x¾″	6x1¼″	8x1¾″	8x2½″
5x¾″	6x1½″	10x1¾″	12x2½″

Here are the sizes and quantities of the common headed nails which are sold by the pound:

Length (in.)	Sizes (d)	No. per lb.
1	2	876
1¼	3	568
1½	4	316
1¾	5	271
2	6	174
2¼	7	161
2½	8	106
2¾	9	96
3	10	69

To do a neat job in cabinet work it is necessary to drill holes for all screws. The first hole, drilled the full length of the screw to take the threaded portion should be ⅟₁₆ inch less in diameter than the hole for the screw shank which is drilled afterwards. The upper hole is then countersunk to bring the slotted head slightly below the surface.

Counterboring consists of drilling a hole the full diameter of the screw head so that the entire screw is sunk deep into the wood. This enables you to use a short screw for fastening a thick piece of wood, and also permits the screw head being buried deep enough to take a wooden plug above it. Such a plug can be either decorative or made to match the grain and so hide the location of the hole. In counterboring, the pilot hole is drilled as before and

used as a guide for the counterbore. There is never any need to drill a separate hole for the screw shank.

In nailing brittle woods and thin pieces it is often safest to make a small hole first to start the nail. This is done with a brad awl. The awl is carefully pushed in, with the flattened end crosswise to the grain, and twisted first to one side, then the other.

On built-in furniture it is sometimes an advantage to use corrugated fasteners to hold joints that are to be hidden. The joints need to be clamped tight before driving in the fastener, otherwise it is best to use the converging type fastener which pulls the two parts together as it enters the wood. Such fasteners are not used in fine cabinet work, but they may be of help in holding and stiffening joints in the frames of built-in pieces.

Glues and Gluing

In any cabinet shop good glue is just as essential as screws for fastening joints. Furthermore it often holds where screws and nails will not.

There are many kinds of glue available, hot, cold, liquid, and powder, but the only kind that you need consider is the modern synthetic resin plastic glue such as Cascamite or Weldwood. This type of glue comes in powder form and is mixed with cold water, a little at a time as needed. Thus there is very little waste and the glue is always fresh. It dries in a couple of hours, and sets thoroughly hard overnight, but the glued joints should be kept in clamps for at least 12 hours and preferably 24, to allow for thorough seasoning of the glue which then attains its maximum strength.

In gluing, the adhesive is mixed to a creamy consistency, and spread thinly over the two contacting surfaces of the joint. The joint is then assembled, and pressure applied. The only exception to clamping is in the application of glue blocks. In this case the joint is freed of air bubbles, and proper contact is assured by rubbing the glued block back and forth in the angle between the two surfaces. No clamp is needed, but if the piece is to be moved about, a small brad judiciously placed may prevent the weight of the block from dislodging it.

In any wood joint, the glue fills the pores of the wood and literally welds the two surfaces together. With the work properly glued and clamped, the joint will become stronger than the surrounding wood so that it cannot be broken apart. The glues mentioned, incidentally, are waterproof when once they have set.

The powdered glues can be bought in small cans, or in five-pound cans which is the most economical way to buy it. However, if you buy the large can, it is best to have a small can with an airtight lid and keep that filled from the large one. In that way the large can is opened less frequently and the contents have less chance of deteriorating from contact with damp air.

Sandpaper

Various grades of abrasive paper are needed for cleaning and smoothing wood surfaces, and removing varnish, paint, or other finish. Ordinary flint paper is not recommended because the particles become so easily detached and embed themselves in the surface of the wood. Probably the most satis-

Stock Sizes of Lumber

Sold as	Actual dimension
1 x 2	¾ x 1⅝
1 x 3	¾ x 2⅝
1 x 4	¾ x 3⅝
1 x 6	¾ x 5⅝
1 x 8	¾ x 7½
1 x 10	¾ x 9½
2 x 2	1⅝ x 1⅝
2 x 4	1⅝ x 3⅝
2 x 6	1⅝ x 5⅝
2 x 8	1⅝ x 7½
2 x 10	1⅝ x 9½
4 x 4	3⅝ x 3⅝

factory abrasive for all-round use on wood is garnet paper. The papers are graded according to the size of the grit, the higher the number the smaller the grit. The sizes most often used in the average cabinet shop are 7/0, 4/0, 2/0, 1/0.

In some work, such as smoothing a shellacked or varnished surface, steel wool may be preferable. This also comes in various degrees of fineness, and the numbers 2/0 and 4/0 are probably the most generally useful.

Cutting and Joining Operations

Chapter IV

Cutting and Joining Operations

Every piece of furniture is designed to serve a certain specific purpose and at the same time withstand wear and tear and accidental damage. In properly designed pieces the normal stresses are distributed and the proportions of the members are calculated to withstand normal strain without being too bulky or heavy.

The proportions of the parts are therefore an important factor in constructing a piece that will withstand more than normal usage, yet look well. Of equal importance is the way those parts are put together. Joints are always potential weak spots, and they must be properly designed and proportioned if they are to add to the strength of the piece instead of detracting from it.

The cabinet maker needs to know how to form all the common, and some uncommon, joints, and also where to use them. Since the making of joints involves a number of simple woodworking operations it may be as well to study them together. Then we shall know not only "how" but "why"—and perhaps better appreciate the reasons behind certain "rule-of-thumb" cabinet-making practices.

There are around twenty kinds of joints used in everyday cabinet making. Of these at least seven are so commonly employed that it is practically essential for every furniture craftsman to be familiar with their construction. Some of these joints have several variations, but only the simplest of these will be discussed here. Others will doubtless be

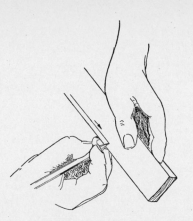

learned automatically as experience widens, and those shown will serve very well to illustrate the principles of joint construction and the practical means of making them.

Marking

A preliminary to any cutting operation is to mark the line along which the cut is to be made. Whether you use a marking gauge, butt gauge, try square, a straightedge, or your fingers, depends upon the location, direction, and shape of the line. But suppose for the moment that you are merely to cut a chamfer along the edge of a board. This is prob-

ably done more for decorative reasons than for fitting, so the line does not have to be exact.

More likely than not you can draw such a line with a sharp pencil by running your fingers down the edge of the board. The pencil is held firmly between thumb and forefinger, and the tips of the third or fourth fingers held lightly against the edge of the board. It is best to draw the pencil toward you and not to move the body during this operation.

Chamfers and Bevels

The sharp corner of the board (called an arris) is removed in chamfering, but the cut does not go the full thickness of the board. Such a full-thickness angle cut would be a bevel. Therefore, in making the chamfer, it is best to mark both the edge and face of the board. The board can then be held in a vise while you plane off the arris down to the lines. If you wish, you can take off the sharp corner first with a spokeshave or drawknife or even a chisel, and finish with the plane.

In cases where the chamfer does not go the full length of the edge but tapers off, it is called a stopped chamfer. In this case you chamfer as much as possible with the plane, and finish off the ends (stops) with a spokeshave or chisel, depending on the shape of the stop.

CHAMFER

BEVEL

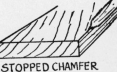

STOPPED CHAMFER

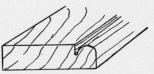

RABBET   BEAD

In making a bevel, only one line need be drawn (on the face or back of the board), and most of the work can be done with a plane. The commonest bevel is 45 degrees, in which case the guide line is marked back from the edge a distance equal to the thickness of the wood.

Beading

Another non-structural operation is that known as beading. It consists, in its simplest form, of forming a round corner in place of an arris, and is often used in conjunction with a chamfer on an adjoining board to make a decorative joint.

The line of the bead is marked off with a pencil as in the case of the chamfer. If the board is short you may be able to make a saw cut along this line, an eighth of an inch or more deep. Then you round off the arris into the saw cut with a plane on the outside and a chisel on the inside of the bead, finishing off with medium sandpaper, preferably glued to a hollowed block. All of this of course takes time and effort, with plenty of opportunities for spoiling the work. It is far better to get yourself a good combination plane with cutters for the sizes of beads that you want most often. With long boards something of the sort is a practical necessity, unless you have a power saw to make the groove.

Rabbets

A common woodworking operation is the forming of a shoulder along the edges or ends of boards or other parts. This operation is known as rabbeting, and involves cutting away a rectangular strip from the ends or edges of the piece.

Rabbets are used as joints between boards, in letting backs, tops, and bottoms into cased pieces, in forming corner joints, and, among other things, in making secret or miter dovetails. The rabbet is marked off for depth and width, i.e., on two adjacent surfaces, and saw cuts made along the line on the face of the board to the depth marked on the

edge. The second cut can also be made with a saw, though on occasion it may be best to use a chisel for both cuts. Ordinarily it is preferable to use a rabbet plane for the job. In that case you set the plane to cut to the required width and do not need to mark the wood except for depth.

Dados

A dado is merely a channel or flat-bottomed groove, and may run either with or across the grain. For example, a dado is cut across boards to receive the ends of shelves, and along the grain to receive drawer bottoms.

There are several variations from the plain dado that goes the full width of a board. Sometimes, for tidy finish, in order to conceal the fact that a shelf is let into the end, the dado is not carried all the way to the front edge of the board. It is then known as a stopped or blind dado.

In another case the shelf may be so thick that it is preferable to rabbet the end to fit a narrower dado channel. The rabbet of course would be from the underside of the shelf, and the result would be a shouldered dado.

Still another variation might be what is called a dovetail dado joint. In this type the dado is cut with one side square as usual, but with the top side undercut at about 45 degrees. The end of the shelf is then cut to fit the dado, and must be slid in from the side. Such a joint prevents the side of the case

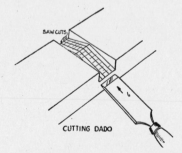

SAW CUTS

CUTTING DADO

from pulling away from the shelf end, and the shelf holds the two sides in position.

Dados are fairly simple to make, especially short ones across the grain. All that is required is a saw cut along each line marking the width of the dado, and some careful use of a chisel to remove the center wood. The chiseling is best done with the work held in a vise, cutting first from one side then the other. The cuts are made from the edges toward the center, the chisel removing less and less as it approaches midpoint. This leaves a triangular piece in the middle after the ends of the slot have been cut down to the finished level. The center portion is then removed, and the bottom of the groove trimmed smooth and even. Cuts should never be made from the center outward—this results in breaking off the bottom edges of the groove.

If you are making a stopped dado, the saw is tilted slightly so that it does not cut beyond the end mark of the slot. The free wood is cut away, and then the slot sides are cut deeper with the chisel.

The blind end of the channel is also chiseled out.

For a dovetail dado the same procedure is followed as for the square one, but the saw is tilted in making the upper saw cut, following a guide line on the edge of the board. This makes the slot wider at the bottom than at the top. The end of the board that fits into this dado is formed by making a saw cut across the upper face and cutting down to it from the end with a chisel. If carefully done it can be sawed at an angle to meet the first saw cut.

If you use a chisel, see that it is extremely sharp. A blunt tool will break off the end grain, spoil the sharp edge, and result in a sloppy fit.

These dadoing operations can be much simplified by using a router plane to remove the waste after the side saw cuts have been made. For those cuts the best tool of all is a bench saw, but if you have such a saw you will doubtless also have a set of dado cutters to use with it and sawing will be unnecessary.

TAPERED DOVETAIL
DADO (STOPPED)

DOVETAIL SHELF
JOINT

DADO

BLIND OR STOPPED
DADO

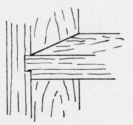
SHOULDERED DADO

BAREFACED DOVETAIL DADO

Glued Joints

An operation frequently called for in cabinet work is the making of narrow boards into wide ones by means of a joint between the two boards, usually one that is not easily detected. In furniture construction, the kind of joint that is made between any two pieces of wood depends primarily on the amount of stress that it must withstand in use. Other factors are the location and direction, or possible concentration of stresses, and the actual strength of

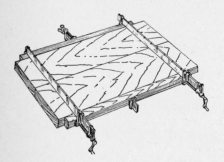

the material itself. It is of little use to make a tremendously strong and heavy joint in wood that itself will break or split easily. Sometimes it is just as well to have joints that give a little under unusual, temporary loads. That may be sufficient to prevent another part breaking.

In joining two boards, the simplest joint is one that is not reinforced in any way. It consists simply of making the adjoining edges of both boards square and smooth, and gluing them together.

The first step is to plane both edges true with the longest plane you have, taking care not to lift it. Place both edges together and see if you can detect light between them at any point. If you do, check that point on each board with a short straightedge, such as a square. Then take a long and very fine plane cut over the high spots that are holding the boards apart at that point, and try again.

When the two boards fit together reasonably well,

apply glue to both edges, and clamp them together tightly. If you have a stiff length of 2 x 2 to place under the clamp jaws on either side of the assembly, so much the better—the pressure will be more evenly distributed. In any case the clamps should not be more than two feet apart on long stock, and one foot is better though not always necessary if you use long clamping blocks or strips. Clamp as tightly as possible without damaging the wood, until all excess glue is forced out of the joint. Excess glue should be wiped off at once, from both sides, with a damp rag.

If you use three or more clamps, place alternate ones on opposite sides of the assembly, and let the bars touch the wood, some on top, some on the bottom. This will help prevent the boards buckling at the joint and keep them flat. If one or the other of the boards tends to get out of line at the ends, use C-clamps or Jorgensens to hold them level and in line.

Some cabinet workers prefer to have the board joints hit at the ends and be slightly hollow in the center—but not more than ½ inch. The theory is that when glued tight there will be no tendency for the ends of the joint to spring apart. Naturally, any board bowed in the oppostie direction (tight at center, open at ends) should not be used in that condition. If properly made with waterproof glue, a glued joint will be stronger than the wood behind it.

This type of joint is used for table and cabinet tops quite successfully. Indeed, any single board wide enough to be used for such a purpose would probably warp. That is why it is common practice to saw such boards into several strips, reverse the alternate ones so that the grain tensions counteract those of the boards on either side of it, and glue the whole together again. In doing this with wood that is to be given a transparent finish it is of course necessary to match up the grain in such a way that the joints are not too obvious.

BLIND DOVETAIL

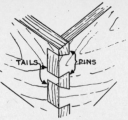

TAILS PINS

THE DOVETAIL JOINT

FRAME DOVETAIL

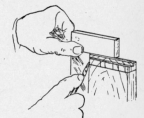

MARKING OUT BLIND DOVETAIL

Spline Joints

A joint for board edges that can be used either with or without glue is the spline joint, sometimes called the slip-tongue or loose-tongue joint. This joint consists of a single groove in the edge of each board into which is fitted a continuous strip of wood. If the joint is not fastened in any way, except for the tight fit of the spline, it can adjust itself to changing moisture conditions. The boards may expand and shrink in width but there will never be an open space between them. This is the principle of the panel, and it is sometimes used for the backs of cabinet pieces. On the other hand the joint can be held lightly with brads driven through both sides of the spline, or the whole firmly glued together.

The first operation in making this joint is to cut the grooves in the edges of the boards. These grooves should not be wider than one-third the thickness of the board. A router plane is almost a necessity in cutting these grooves, unless the pieces are very short so that a back saw and chisel can be used. With a bench saw, of course, the operation is simple.

The grooves, ordinarily, are not deeper than about half the thickness of the wood. Cutting the spline therefore involves little more than sawing off a strip of wood from the edge of a board of the required thickness, and smoothing it sufficiently to make a snug fit in the grooves. Very often, a few passes with a sanding block will do the trick. The finished strip should not be too wide to permit the joint being tightly closed.

Tongue-and-Groove Joints

A tongue-and-groove joint consists of a continuous flat strip or tongue along the edge of one board, designed to fit into a groove in the edge of another board. For most purposes this is a much more satisfactory joint than the spline type, but it is even harder to make with ordinary hand tools. However, you can buy, at quite moderate cost, a tongue-and-groove match plane designed for just such work. One side of the plane makes the tongue, the other side the groove, and each will fit the other perfectly. The joint can be made with a bench saw, but great care is needed to work on the waste side of the dimension lines and so get a tight fit. A loose tongue-and-groove joint is worse than none at all.

Dowel Joints

It was mentioned above that glued-edge joints, properly made, are stronger than the surrounding wood. One possible effect of this would be that any excessive bearing stress on the joint might snap the wood on either side of it. Any such stress could be spread over a larger area if the wood on either side of the joint were reinforced. This is exactly what happens when dowels are used in conjunction with the glue. With wood that cracks easily they are almost a necessity.

Dowels are merely short round pieces of rod, of

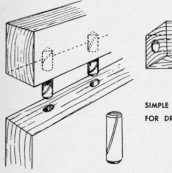

SIMPLE DEPTH GAUGE
FOR DRILLING HOLES

maple, birch, or beech. Dowels three or four inches long are smeared with glue and pushed into paired holes in the edges of boards, and the two boards are clamped together as usual. But fitting dowels is not so simple as it may sound. The dowel holes in the two board edges have to be perfectly aligned and quite parallel with the board surfaces.

The first step in doweling, then, is to make a center line along the edge of one of the boards, and mark thereon the center for the dowel holes. The next important thing is to make sure that the holes you are about to drill will be exactly opposite the holes you have to drill in the edge of the other board. There are several ways of doing this, and each cabinet maker has his own favorite method.

You can mark the center on both boards at once with a try square while they are held, edge-up, in a vise. You can drill the holes in one side, and insert in them wooden pegs or metal discs that have a sharp point sticking out of their center. If you now bring the boards together, with the hole center marks exactly in line, the points will puncture the unmarked board at the drilling centers.

Other craftsmen favor marking both boards and using a doweling jig. We prefer to mark both sets of centers at once by driving short brads into the pencil-marked centers on one board edge. The heads of these brads (projecting less than an eighth of an inch) are then nipped off leaving a tiny metal point.

Now both boards are laid close together on a perfectly flat surface and exactly in line. The edges are pressed together so the points in one pierce the other board. Separating the two boards you remove the brads. This leaves two sets of matching holes marking the centers for the drill. Of course it is still necessary to see that the holes are drilled perpendicular to the two edges, and that they are the exact depth required.

Drilling straight without a jig requires a keen eye and a steady wrist, and constant checking with a try square. If you have no doweling jig you can improvise one with clamps and blocks of wood.

The dowel itself needs to be chamfered slightly so that it will slide easily into the holes. Some workers also slightly countersink the holes, but this is rarely necessary. The dowel also should have one or more grooves cut along its length. This can be done with a saw or a triangular file, or even a chisel. Its purpose is to release air and excess glue when forcing the dowels into the holes.

When the depth of the dowel holes is decided upon, a bit gauge is clamped to the drill at that point. If you have no gauge you can quickly make one by drilling a hole through a small block of wood that will extend from the brace chuck and leave only the desired length of drill exposed. Make the dowel itself about ⅛ inch shorter than the combined depths of the two holes.

The dowels can be driven into one set of holes with a mallet, but you may need to draw the two boards together with clamps to get the dowel ends into the other set of holes. In any case they should be left in clamps until the glue is set so that you will have a good edge joint as well as a good dowel joint.

Mortise-and-Tenon Joints

One of the best-known of all furniture joints is the mortise-and-tenon. It is used to connect two pieces more or less at right angles to one another. In its simplest form it consists of a tongue (tenon) cut on the end of one piece which is held in a rectangular hole through the other piece. If the hole (mortise) does not go all the way through the wood, the joint is called a blind tenon, but the principle is the same.

In making this joint the marking out is vitally important. Mark out the mortise first, the exact height of the tenon stock, and square the lines right around the mortise member. Then, with a marking gauge (or with a mortise gauge which marks two

lines at once) inscribe the two vertical lines that indicate the width of the mortise. That width should be one-third the thickness of the piece that is to form the tenon.

Presuming that the tenon piece is exactly the same thickness as the mortised member, use the gauge setting to mark out the tenon, top, bottom, and end. But first run a line around the tenon piece at a distance from its end equal to the thickness of the mortise member plus ¹⁄₁₆ inch or slightly more. This extra length provides for smoothing and leveling off the tenon end later.

Having checked all these dimensions against one another you are ready to begin cutting. Select an augur bit slightly smaller than the width of the mortise and drill a series of holes where the mortise is to be. With much of the waste thus removed, you can cut out the rest with a chisel and mallet. Work from the middle to the ends, making vertical cuts every quarter-inch or so, and finish inside the end line. Dig out the waste wood and repeat till you are at least halfway through, then turn the piece over and work from the other side.

If you are careful and keep your chisel up straight, the hole will not need trimming at the sides. If you have wandered outside the guide lines you can allow for this in making the tenon. That is why the mortise is cut first.

Use your back saw to cut the tenon, starting at the end and working down to the shoulder. The piece is held in the vise for this operation, and care must be taken to keep the saw along, but outside, the lines. The tenon is finished by laying the piece in the bench hook and cutting the waste off both sides. Be very careful to follow the lines here, otherwise one shoulder will not be snug against the mortise and the joint can rock, besides looking sloppy. The tenon can be trimmed slightly with a chisel if it fits too snugly on first trial.

In most of the mortised joints used in cabinet work the tenon is also shouldered top and bottom.

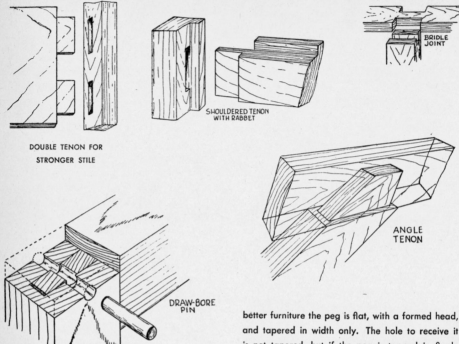

DOUBLE TENON FOR
STRONGER STILE

SHOULDERED TENON
WITH RABBET

BRIDLE
JOINT

ANGLE
TENON

DRAW-BORE
PIN

This makes a joint that is stiffer vertically, provided it is properly proportioned. In most old-time work and much of the new, when a thinner rail tenons into a thicker leg, the front of the rail is made flush with the front of the leg. This is a very important point to watch in dealing with antique reproductions. It has the practical advantage of keeping two tenons entering the same leg at right angles to one another the maximum distance apart. The result is a stronger leg at the mortises.

If the joint is to be used on knock-down pieces, the tenon is made longer and a hole cut through it to receive a peg. This is also done on fixed pieces when the design calls for it. On cheaper units the peg is often put through the side of the tenon and may be round or half-round and tapered. On the better furniture the peg is flat, with a formed head, and tapered in width only. The hole to receive it is not tapered, but if the peg is tapped in firmly it will not move.

Quite often a tenon is made so that it does not go all the way through the mortised piece. Such a blind tenon is made in almost exactly the same way as the full tenon, but with the mortises cut not deeper than three-quarters of the way through. To drill out such a mortise it is generally safest to use a Forstner bit which has no screw point to break through if you drill too far.

Panel Joints

In constructing the backs of cased pieces it is often necessary to make a frame to receive flat panels. The joints used here are either the full (through) or blind tenons, or what is known as an open tenon. The joint is complicated by the fact that all rails are either rabbeted or grooved to receive the panel. In the case of a rabbet, one side of the tenon is made in the usual way. The other side, which incorporates the rabbet is cut back sufficiently to accommodate the rabbet on the mortised stile. If a groove is used both sides are cut back. In neither instance is the top of the tenon shouldered—it remains level with the bottom of the rabbet or groove.

In the case of a top rail the tenon has to be shouldered on the upper side so that the mortise will not come too close to the end of the stile. Merely narrowing the tenon would leave a gap between the upper rail end and the stile because of the groove in the latter. This gap is closed by keeping the tenon the full width as far as the bottom of the groove. The reduced width of the tenon where it enters the mortise leaves a projection that is referred to as a haunch. Besides filling gaps, haunches on tenons also provide an extra bearing surface that strengthens the rail against twisting. This idea is sometimes incorporated in top rails that fit into legs or other vertical members. In these cases the mortise is made in the usual way. Then a shallow slot is cut through from the mortise to the top of the member. This slot is the same width as the mortise but it may be no more than ¾ inch deep. This slot serves to accommodate the tenon haunch.

The rail on which the tenon is to be cut is of course wide enough to extend from the bottom of the mortise to the top of the leg. The tenon, on the other hand, has to be rabbeted on the top side to fit the mortise. This rabbet is not made level with the side shoulders but a certain distance in front of them. This distance should be equal to the depth of the slot. The projecting piece of tenon, which was not cut away, then forms the required haunch.

The open mortise joint mentioned earlier is similar in construction to the through mortise, but it is made at the end of a stile, and an open-sided slot takes the tenon instead of a regular mortise. This joint is very easy to make since the slot can be cut with a saw and the waste chiseled out. But, naturally, it is not as strong as a regular mortise joint, and the tenon needs to be pinned in position. On the better cabinet pieces the open tenon is not used where the open end of the joint is exposed and can be seen.

Leg Tenons

In rare cases where the leg is too thin to take a pair of ordinary tenons at right angles to one another it may be necessary to miter the tenons. This makes a stronger joint than cutting the tenons square and short, but it is not a joint to be attempted by the inexperienced. This kind of joint also can be stiffened by adding the haunch described before.

If a tenon joint has to be made between two pieces that are at more, or less, than 90 degrees to one another, the construction is somewhat different. One face of the tenon remains level, i.e., parallel with the piece it is formed on. The other is cut to enter the mortise at right angles to the face of the mortised piece. The tenon therefore has one sloping side, and the mortise must be cut to suit. This all calls for careful marking out before any cuts are made.

The subject of tenons cannot be left without brief reference to draw-boring. A great many tenons are pinned by driving a short piece of dowel into a hole through the joint. In order that the two parts of the joint shall be pulled together as tighly as possible in pinning, the hole in the tenon is sometimes drilled ⅟₁₆ inch or so nearer the shoulder than the mortise pin holes. When the joint is assembled, a slightly tapered dowel is driven through, thereby pulling all the holes into line and tightening the joint.

Dovetail Joints

Dovetail joints are made in various forms but the principle of them all is that of interlocking tapers.

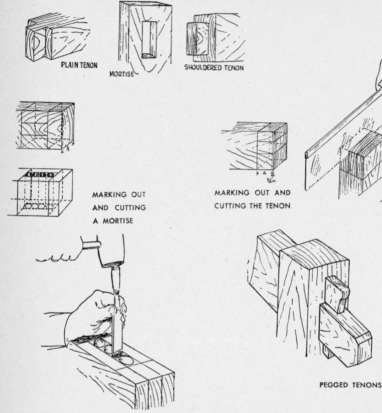

PLAIN TENON

MORTISE

SHOULDERED TENON

MARKING OUT
AND CUTTING
A MORTISE

MARKING OUT AND
CUTTING THE TENON

PEGGED TENONS

Dovetails are essentially corner joints. The single dovetail is like an open mortise-and-tenon, but the tenon is wedge-shaped so that it cannot pull out. The tenon is called the pin, and the mortise is called the socket. The wood between each pair of sockets is the dovetail—or, simply, the tail.

In constructing dovetail joints the pins are always made first, and the sockets marked out from them (The reverse of the tenon joint procedure). In the early days the pins were small and the tails large,

and a few of them were use to a joint. Later construction favored more equal tails and pins, and all of them large. The present fashion is for many dovetails, with the pins much smaller than the tails.

When the pins and the tails are the same size the joint is known as a cistern dovetail. This design makes a very strong joint, and one that is least affected by shrinkage or expansion of the wood. It is, however, not essential for ordinary cabinet pieces.

Some cabinet makers gauge the size of the dovetail members according to the hardness or softness of the wood. In a hard wood the root of the pin

BAREFACED TENON WITH PANEL GROOVE

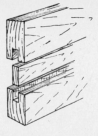

HAUNCHED TENON JOINT
WITH PANEL GROOVES

SPLINE JOINT TONGUE & GROOVE

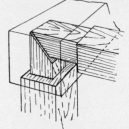

SHOULDERED TENONS INTO CORNER POSTS
(IN LINE WITH OUTER FACES)

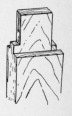

MITERED TENONS

can usually be thinner than it can in a soft wood, but under ordinary conditions this is not of great importance.

The proportions of the pins will depend upon the circumstances (kind and thickness of wood, length of joint, etc.) but a good rule-of-thumb system is to make the wider face of the pins equal to, or very slightly less than, the thickness of the wood. In most cases the angle to which the sides of the pins are cut is about 10 degrees to the center line or 80 degrees to the base.

The dovetails used for drawer fronts are known as blind dovetails because they do not extend through the front of the drawer and therefore cannot be seen from that point. In the case of these dovetails the pins are usually made a little thinner, but they should never be less than $\frac{3}{16}$ inch at their thinnest part. The end pins on the drawers of course have only one sloped side and are, in effect, half pins. In their case it is necessary to

strengthen them by thickening them slightly. This is allowed for in marking out as described later.

Cutting the ordinary "through" dovetail joint is a simple matter once the pins and tails are marked out, but great precision is called for. A sloppy fit will ruin the joint. The common dovetail has the pins spaced quite far apart, the tails often being an inch or more wide. It is therefore a good joint to practice on.

The first step is to prepare the two pieces of wood, cutting and smoothing to finished dimensions. The ends of the pieces also are planed off square for marking, but should be left $\frac{1}{2}$ to $\frac{1}{16}$ inch long for smoothing after the joint is made.

Starting with the piece that will form the pins, the end is marked around with the square at a distance equal to the thickness of the other piece that will form the sockets plus the excess that you have allowed. Now you will have to decide how many pins you are going to use, remembering that they should not be less than $\frac{1}{4}$ inch thick at their roots. If you decide on $\frac{1}{4}$ inch add $\frac{1}{16}$ to the thickness of the end pins, and mark that distance off

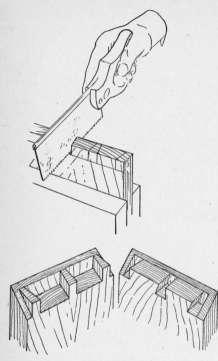

CUTTING THE BLIND PINS &
DOVETAILS ON A DRAWER

MITRE DOVETAIL

along the proper edge. Then you will be able to gauge the number of full-sized pins you can get between the end ones, allowing about twice the thickness of the pins for the tails.

Having measured off these points, set your bevel to 80 degrees or thereabouts and draw the lines on the end grain of the wood to indicate the ends of the pins. In marking, use a sharp knife or pencil, or fine-pointed awl. Then, laying the board flat, use a square to extend those lines to the base line first drawn. Do this on both sides of the board and you will have an outline of each pin.

The pins are cut out by putting the board vertically in a vise and sawing down to the base line. To get a tight fit keep the saw on the waste side of the lines. If the end pins are not too thin you

can cut out all the waste wood between them with a chisel. Lay the work flat and cut from one side; then turn it over and finish from the other side. The spaces can be cleaned up with a paring chisel.

With the pins finished you can now use them to mark out the sockets, being sure that the pins are turned with their narrower faces toward the end of the board. Scribe around them carefully, then saw down the vertical sides. Cut the half-sockets out with the tenon saw, but use a chisel to remove the waste from the whole sockets. If the marking out is done with precision, and the cuts made on the waste sides of the lines, the two parts of the joint should go together in a tight push fit.

This matter of careful cutting is the whole secret of good dovetail joints. You will find that in laying out you do not need to go to extremes to get all pins or tails exactly the same size as one another. An approximation is sufficient provided the fit is good.

In the fronts of drawers the dovetails must be of

the blind variety. This joint is a little more trouble to make than the common dovetail, especially in the cutting. In these joints you can make the pins smaller, but the end half-pins need to be thickened by about an eighth of an inch. Here again you cut the pins first (they are formed in the drawer front), but instead of cutting them through the full thickness of the board you leave an eighth or more to hide the ends of the tails. Therefore, in cutting you hold the drawer front firmly in a vise, end up, and, after marking out the pins, saw through the arris at an angle till the saw teeth just reach the front and top marking lines. Here you need to be extremely careful not to saw too deep and mar the end wood.

Having sawn on both sides of the center pins and one side of the end half-pins, you take the board from the vise and lay it on the bench, back up. Now you can chisel out the waste as far as possible. The triangular portion left in the sockets will have to be cut with a chisel. Some of this will need to be done with the work held vertically in the vise again. With the pins finally cleaned down to the lines by paring, you can use them to mark out the tails as before.

There are a number of other dovetails types, but the two described are commonest and easily mastered. More intricate ones such as the miter dovetail are not used on ordinary furniture except for special purposes. When you have become thoroughly familiar with the making of the plain blind dovetails you can tackle the miter form with confidence. From the drawing you can see exactly how it is made.

Miter Cutting

A miter is a cut made at an angle to the surface of the wood, or, more technically, bevelling the ends of two pieces of wood in order to join them at an angle. In 90-degree joints the miter is cut at 45 degrees on the two ends that fit together. The line of the joint is then visible only along the corner arris that the two boards form.

The cutting of such miters is much simplified by the use of a miter box. You can make a very simple one by nailing three boards together to form a trough, and making saw cuts (kerfs) through the two upstanding sides at the required angle. The 45-degree angle is easily marked with the aid of a carpenter's square. You merely hold the square flat on top of the two parallel edges of the trough so that the same inch marks on both arms of the square touch the same edges. You can also use a

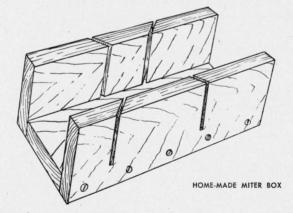

HOME-MADE MITER BOX

SECRET TENON MITRE

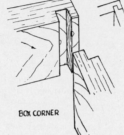

HALVED MITRE

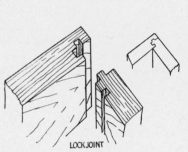

CUT OFF FLUSH

MITRE FILLET

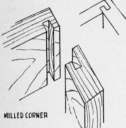

MILLED CORNER

BOX CORNER

LOCK JOINT

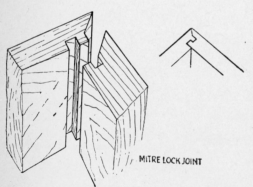

MITRE LOCK JOINT

metal miter box, either of the fixed or adjustable type. With the latter you can set any angle you require.

After cutting the miters you can glue the two faces together but you should have ready some means of clamping the parts in position. Metal miter clamps are available, but for many jobs you can make a satisfactory clamp by screwing a wood block to a heavy board base. This block must have a large, right-angled notch cut out of one edge to form a 90-degree inside corner. A triangular block is placed in this angle which it fits exactly.

To use this device the two halves of the miter are placed together in the angle of the fixed block, and the triangular one put inside the miter. Any suitable clamp is made to straddle both blocks and tightened. This forces the triangular block tightly into the angle. The friction between it and the work while tightening presses the miter joint parts together and holds them there firmly.

combination square for this, marking each edge in turn with the 45-degree surface. The mark is continued to the second board edge with a straightedge. If the wood is over an inch thick you may be able to use a miter box with one side only because the kerf will be long enough to guide the back saw properly. It is of course much better to invest in a

On some pieces of work, where a hole in one side does not matter, you can put a screw in the wood each side of the joint, clamp the pieces flat to a board, and pull the joint together with a clamp on the screws. Better still is a small block screwed to each of the pieces. There is also a clamp made for professional use that holds the parts together with a pair of stub fingers that fit into holes in the wood.

In addition to the plain joint you can use the dovetail miter previously described; you can dowel the miter, screw or nail it (preferably after gluing) or use a loose fillet or spline, or even hold it together with a keyed dovetail. You can also make a mitered half-lap joint, a secret tenon, or a dovetail tenon. The illustrations make the construction of these joints clear; the rest is a matter of accurately making and cutting as in the case of the other joints described in detail.

There are many other possible joints for corners, some of which are interlocking. The first advance over a plain rabbet joint combines a dado and a rabbet and is known as a box corner. This is not recommended, especially in thin wood, because the dado is made of necessity close to the end and across the grain so that it is extremely weak. The same thing applies to the milled corner joint which combines two dadoes and a rabbet (or a dado, tongue, and rabbet). These joints should be used only with hard, tough woods, and where no great strain will be imposed upon them.

Somewhat better is the lock joint which combines three dadoes with two tongues. This can only be assembled by sliding one piece sidewise into the other, therefore all dimensions must be absolutely accurate and the surface perfectly straight. It is not a joint to make by hand. The lock miter joint is simpler, merely having a tongue that fits into an end dado with the outer edges mitered.

Corner Blocks

Where possible, all mechanically weak joints of any variety should be reinforced with corner blocks. These can be triangular or square in section and preferably held with glue. The beginner, however,

MITRE CLAMP

should confine his joint-making to tenons and dovetails, unless he has a shop fully equipped with precision power tools and has considerable skill himself.

Details for Making Articles

Chapter V

Details for Making Articles

A. MOVABLE FURNITURE

SCONCE

Wood: Pine.

Material Requirements:

> Back—One piece ⅜" x 5½" x 12¼".
> Base—One piece ⅜" x 5" x 7⅝".
> Sides—Two pieces ⅜" x 3⅜ x 8¼" (two sides can be
> cut from one piece 4⅓ x 8¼"').

Procedure:

This is a simple fret saw (or jig saw) job, and in shaping the wood only the dimensions of the back are of vital importance. Lay out the shape on a piece of wood by using ½" or 1". squares as shown. The sweep of the shoulders will determine whether the sconce is handsome or not. The shapes of the sides or wings are not critical as long as they have a flowing sweep to them.

Cut out roughly all four pieces, and check by holding together in position. This will also give you an idea of how much to cut away from the back outside edges of the wings to enable them to fit flush to the back at the proper angle. Assemble the base to the back first, with glue and brads, then add the wings. Note that the wings do not have to be exactly in line with the edges of the base. Sand off all arrises.

This is an old-time piece and a few small irregularities will add to the antique air, especially if it is given the antique pine finish described elsewhere.

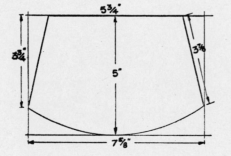

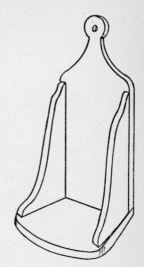

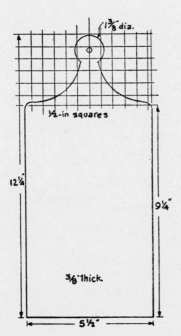

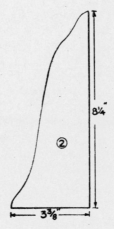

PIPE BOX

Wood: Pine.

Material Requirements:

> Back—One piece ⅜" x 4¾" x 17¼".
> Sides—Two pieces ⅜" x 5⅝" x 12⅛.
> Front—One piece ⅜" x 4¾" x 7".
> Base—One piece ¾" x 4⅛" x 5¼".
> Partition—One piece ⅜" x 3⅛" x 4".
> Drawer—(Front) One piece ½" x 2½" x 4¾"; (back)
> one piece ⅜" x 2½" x 3½"; (sides) two pieces ¼"
> x ¾" x 2½'; (bottom) one piece ¼" x 3⅛" x 3½".
> Knob—Wood, clothespin type, ⅜" diameter for ⁵⁄₁₆"
> hole.

Procedure:

Ordinarily made to hold long-stemmed "church-warden" clay pipes, this box hangs in many a hall to hold a clothes brush, with car keys in the drawer. This modern application governs the dimensions to some extent, but the proportion should be adhered to. The back is cut out first, and the shape of the neck and handle can be outlined on squared paper which is then pasted to the wood. Note the shoulders are recessed to take the sides which are glued and nailed on. The two sides are cut out while clamped or bradded together so that the curves are alike. The exact shape of the upper part is not critical but should not be awkward, so follow the drawing as closely as possible.

After assembling the sides to the back, insert the partition, which should fit snugly on all three sides and be set in ⅛" across the front. Its bottom surface must be a hair's breadth above the lower lip of the box front, and it must be set in absolutely square or the drawer will bind. For this reason it is best to locate it by marking the inner faces of the sides with a line square to the front edges, before installing them. Four brads should be sufficient for each side, and two ½" brads through the back, near the sides, and one brad through each side near the front edge, should hold the partition firmly in place.

The front is next fitted. This is ⅜" material, but

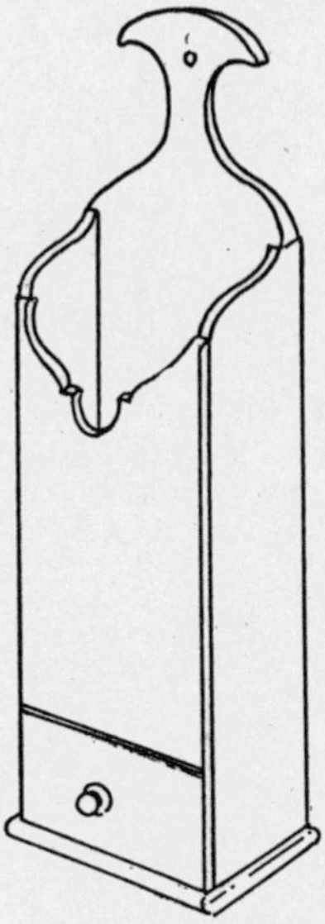

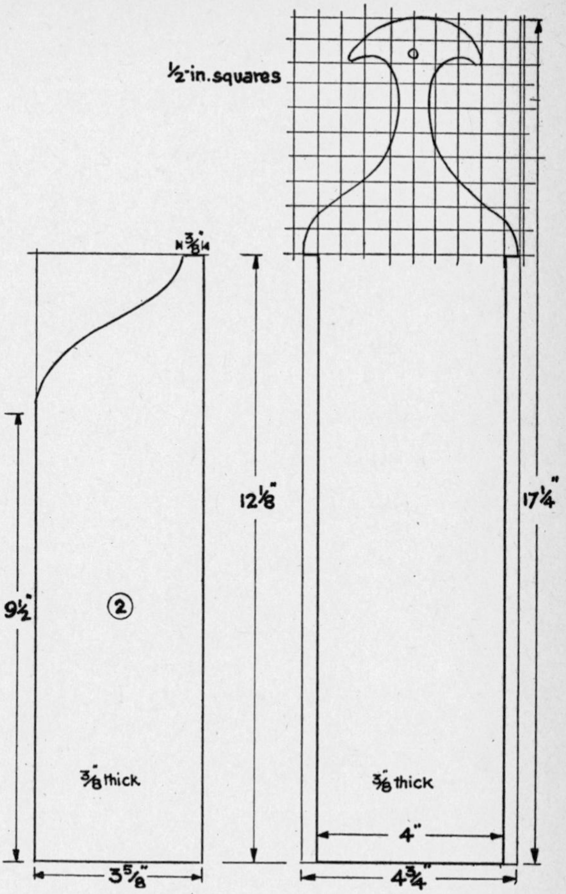
½" in. squares
⅜"
9½"
12⅛"
17¼"
2
⅜" thick
⅜" thick
4"
3⅝"
4¾"

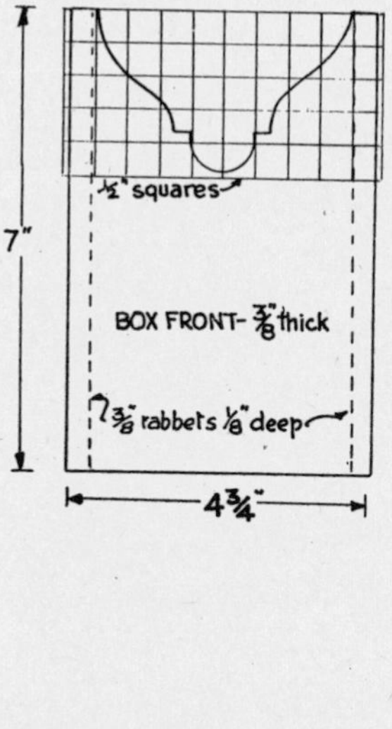
½" squares
7"
BOX FRONT- ⅜" thick
⅜" rabbets ⅛" deep
4¾"

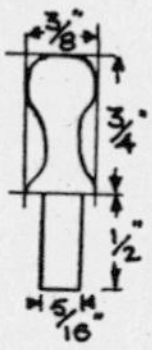
⅜"
¾"
½"
5/16"

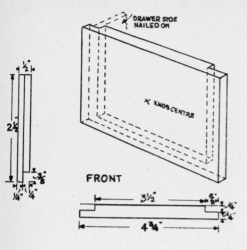

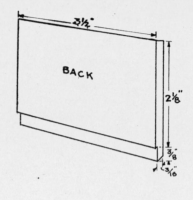

FRONT

BACK

(NOT TO SCALE)

the two vertical edges are rabbeted the thickness of the box sides (⅜″) to a depth of ⅛″. Edges, ¼″ thick, therefore show at the sides of the box. The upper edges of the front where they fit against the sides pieces are later sanded off to minimize the break between the two lines.

The base is attached last, flush at the back, but projecting ¼″ at front and sides. These edges are sanded round. Finally the drawer is made and fitted. The drawer front is rabbeted to take the sides, that are glued and nailed to it, and also to extend over the sides of the box. The sides are made the full depth of the drawer front, but the front itself is rabbeted at the lower edge to accom-

modate the drawer bottom. The back of the drawer also is made the full depth of the front and rabbeted to receive the bottom. The front and back rabbets being ⅜″ deep and the bottom ¼″ thick, the bottom is set in ⅛″. It is fastened in place with a couple of brads driven through it into the front and back rabbets, after gluing, and one through each side into the bottom. This unorthodox method copies an original old-timer (except for the glue). The modern way would be to cut grooves in front and sides for the bottom to slide in, and finish the back above the bottom. However, this decreases the inside depth of he drawer considerably, an important matter in such a shallow drawer as this.

HANGING BOOKSHELF

Wood: Pine.

Material Requirements:

> Sides—Two pieces ¾" x 7" x 38".
> Shelves—Two pieces ¾" x 6½" x 28"; one piece
> ¾" x 7" x 28".
> Braces—Two pieces ½" x 2" x 28¾".

Procedure:

Cut three shelves, and match exactly for length and squareness. Cut two side pieces to length and width. Mark out and cut right-hand side to shape. Lay this on left side and mark around as guide in cutting ends to same shape. On inside of left-hand piece, mark off positions of dadoes according to squared diagram. Use this diagram as a guide in marking out curves between dadoes. Next use left-hand piece as guide in locating dadoes on right-hand side piece. Cut dadoes in both pieces, and fit shelf ends to them. Use narrow shelves top and bottom, all three being flush with the front edges of sides. Behind top and bottom shelves, mark cut-out for the braces. Then cut braces to fit snugly. After assembling dry for fit, glue shelf ends to one side, and hold with two screws each, counterbored, and later plugged. Attach other side similarly, checking finally for squareness. Then insert braces, glue and screw to ends and also to backs of upper and lower shelves. Finish with thorough sanding.

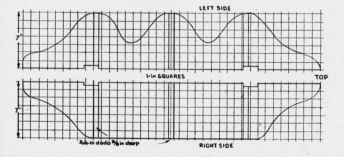

LEFT SIDE

1-in SQUARES

TOP

¾-in dado ⅜-in deep

RIGHT SIDE

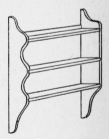

STANDING BOOKSHELF

Wood: Pine, oak or maple.

Material Requirements:

> Ends—Two pieces ¾" x 9" x 38¾" (since these taper
> to 7", the two can be cut from one board 16⅛"
> wide).
> Shelves—One piece ¾" x 9" x 42"; one piece ¾" x
> 8¼" x 42"; one piece ¾" x 7¾" x 42"; one piece
> ¾" x 7¼" x 42".
> Top—One piece ¾" x 7" x 42".
> Back—One piece ¼" x 37¼" x 40½" (ply).
> Base—Two pieces 2½" x 2½" x 42"; two pieces 2½"
> x 2½" x 9".

Procedure:

Mark out and make the ends first, squaring the shelf positions from the back edges (the front edge tapers). Note that there is a shallow dado to receive each shelf in addition to the mortises. This need not be more than ⅛" deep. Cut mortises after dadoing, but do not make dovetail pins till dovetails are cut in top and bottom board ends. Note the inside shelves are set in ½" from the back to allow for the backboard. Cut tenons on shelf end about ⅛₆" narrower than mortises to allow for later insertion of wedges. Next cut dovetails on top and bottom pieces, and from them cut the pins. Cut the back to fit, and absolutely square, then assemble the shelves to the ends with glue; assemble top and bottom boards, also glued, and insert the backboard to square up the whole structure, checking with a steel square. Thin, glued wedges are now driven into the mortise joints, and the top and bottom boards are clamped 24 hours till the glue sets.

Meanwhile make the base, which is simply mitered and held with a glued feather at each corner. This is attached to the bottom of the shelf assembly by screws driven down through the bottom board into the base members. If other than plywood is used for the back, or if there is any danger of shrinkage, it would be best to rabbet the top and bottom boards and the two ends to receive the back board. The back would then need to be ¾" wider and higher to fit a ⅜" rabbet.

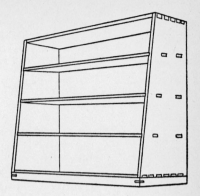

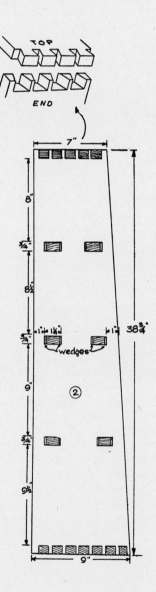

TOP

END

7"

8"

¾"

8½"

¾"

1" · 1⅛" · · 1"

wedges

②

9"

¾"

9½"

38¾"

9"

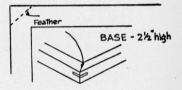

Feather

BASE - 2½" high

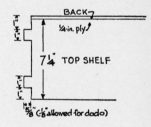

BACK

¼ in. ply

7¼" TOP SHELF

⅝" (⅛ allowed for dado)

CUTLERY TRAY

Wood: Pine, or mahogany, or walnut.

Material Requirements:

> Sides—Two pieces ⁵⁄₁₆″ x 1⅞″ x 10⅜″.
> Ends—Two pieces ⁵⁄₁₆″ x 3¼″ x 8″.
> Handle—One piece ⅝″ x 3⅝″ x 11″.
> Base—One piece ⅜″ x 7″ x 10⅝″.

Procedure:

The principal difficulties with this piece lie in securing the correct angles between the joints, but much of this is a matter of trial and adjustment. The sides slope outward and must be trimmed to sit flat on the base. The ends likewise lean outward and the shoulders must be flat on the sides to give a close joint. All of this calls for careful trimming and fitting. The rest is a matter of layout and cutting to shape. Usually it is best to make the handle unit first, paying attention to the angle of the ends which will determine the slope of the end pieces. The ends are made next, allowing ⅛″ on the depth for trimming flat after gluing and bradding to the handle, but no attaching should be done till all parts are ready for assembly.

The angle of the handle ends will serve as a guide for laying out the end angles of the side pieces.

These pieces also should have an extra ⅛″ for trimming after assembly; only the center (handle) piece does not, because it sits squarely, at right angles, on the base. The five upper pieces are carefully put together, glued, and bradded before that unit is attached to the base. All trimming of the bottom edges is therefore done at the same time.

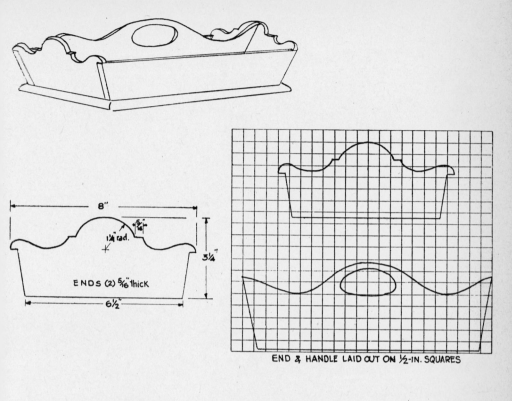

8"

5/8"

1¼" rad.

ENDS (2) 5/16" thick

3¾"

6½"

END & HANDLE LAID OUT ON ½-IN. SQUARES

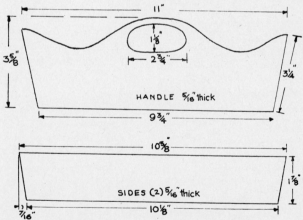

11"

1⅛"

2¾"

3⅝"

3¼"

HANDLE 5/16" thick

9¾"

10⅜"

1⅛"

SIDES (2) 5/16" thick

7/16"

10⅛"

SPICE BOX LAMP BASE

Wood: Pine.

Material Requirements:

> Sides—Two pieces ¾" x 4½" x 17".
> Spacers—Three pieces ⅞" x 3" x 3⅜"; (bottom) one
> piece 1⅛" x 3" x 3¾".
> Top—One piece ¾" x 4½" x 4½".
> Moulding—(Base moulding) 2 ft. 2" of 1"; strip mould-
> ing) 5 ft. of ½"; (crown moulding) 2 ft. of ¾".
> Drawers—Five dummies ¼" x 3¼" x 3⅜"; (fronts)
> three pieces ⅝" x 3½" x 3½"; (backs) three pieces
> ¼" x 2¼" x 2¾"; (sides) six pieces ¼" x 3" x 3½";
> (bottoms) three pieces 3⁄16" x 2½" x 2⅞".
> Brass Knobs—Eight ⅜".

Procedure:

Sides, back, and spacers are first assembled with glue and brads, and the top, first shaped and drilled through, is glued, and nailed on. This top piece is let into the sides and back which are rabbeted to half their thickness. At the front this cap finishes flush with the side members. Note that the three central spacers are ⅛" short. This is to give a clearance of ⅛" between the back of the spacer and the back of the box for the electric cord.

Otherwise the spacers can be notched for the same purpose, but the slots simplify the electrical work. All this material is heavy to give the base solidity. Observe that there are only three usable drawers. Those on the back are all dummies to match the front ones in appearance. The top front one likewise is a dummy, the top spacer being drilled and counterbored to support the brass lamp stem which is held by a nut. Underside of this spacer also is slotted to take the lamp cord and keep it from interfering with the operation of that drawer. The cord then passes down behind the other spacers and emerges at the back through the lower chamfer of the bottom dummy drawer-front.

This base will look well with a shade 14" square and 11¼" high on a standard projecting 8½" above the top cap. The mouldings used on the piece are not critical; anything heavy enough and not too ornate will do.

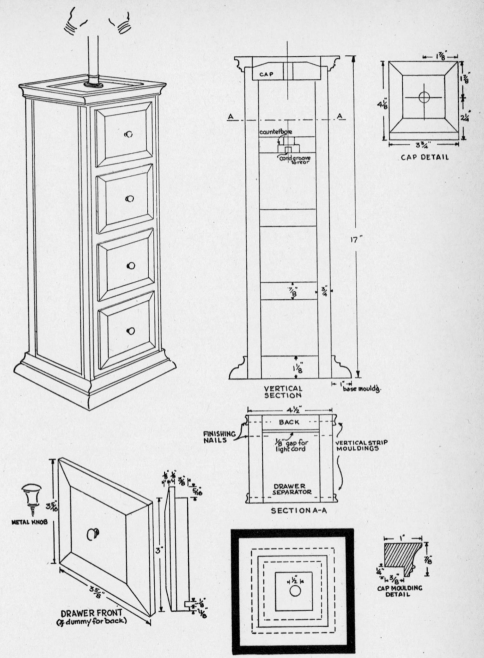

CAP

CAP DETAIL

1⅞"

1⅞"

4⅛"

2¼"

3¾"

A   A

counterbore

cord groove
to rear

17"

⅞"   ¾"

1⅛"

VERTICAL
SECTION

1" base mouldg.

4½"

BACK

FINISHING
NAILS

⅛" gap for
light cord

VERTICAL STRIP
MOULDINGS

DRAWER
SEPARATOR

SECTION A-A

METAL KNOB

3⁵⁄₁₆"

3"

⅜"

¼" ⁵⁄₁₆"

⅛"
¼"

3⅝"

DRAWER FRONT
(& dummy for back)

4½"

1"

⅞"

¼" ³⁄₈"

CAP MOULDING
DETAIL

SAWBUCK COFFEE TABLE

Wood: Pine throughout.

Material Requirements:

Top—One piece ¾" x 18" x 42" (or two narrower pieces jointed and glued together as described in Chapter IV).

Gallery—One piece ⅜" x 2½" x 41"; two pieces ⅜" x 2½" x 16¾".

Cleats—Two pieces 1¼" x 3" x 16¾".

Legs—Four pieces 1¼" x 3" x 22" (cut to shape so that assembly is 18" high).

Stretcher—One piece 1¼" x 2½" x 42".

Pegs—Two pieces ½" x 1½" x 2¾".

Procedure:

Cut each piece to shape and dimensions shown. The finished top, made first, will form a guide for other dimensions.

To make top of single board, saw square, plane face smooth, round corners slightly by sanding; sand off all edges, and smooth them.

To make top from two boards, form straight edge on each board with jointer or longest plane available. Glue and clamp these edges together in line. After 24 hours remove clamps, scrape off surplus glue, and plane top surface (face) smooth and level. Form corners, remove edges, and sand smooth as before.

For the gallery, plane three pieces smooth and of equal thickness. Cut dovetail pins at both ends of long piece. Put end pieces in vise and mark off shape of pins on square end of each. Also mark off thickness of back strip (⅜") to indicate depth of socket. Cut sockets by sawing sides and cutting out with chisel. Work inside socket lines to get tight fit. Round off other ends of sides as shown, by sawing off corner and sanding to a nice curve.

There are several ways in which the legs can be marked off to the proper dimensions and angles, but probably the simplest is to assemble each pair inside a rectangular frame. This frame is made by nailing strips of wood to a flat surface such as a floor or bench or an old batten door. In this case you need four pieces nailed down so as to from a rectangle measuring 18" high and 16½" wide. The corners must be exact right angles (90 degrees). The legs are cut from 3" wide pieces, 1¼" thick and 22" long.

First lay one of these leg pieces cornerwise across the rectangle, with the right-hand corner of the top and the left-hand corner of the bottom in line with the corner of the frame as shown. Holding the leg piece firmly in position, set your bevel protractor blade in line with the frame, top and bottom, and mark off each in turn. You can now continue the pencil mark around the top and bottom, and saw exactly along the lines. This will enable the leg to be slipped snugly into the frame; it should fit into both corners exactly.

Using the first leg as a pattern, mark off the second leg, top and bottom, and cut to shape. Put the first leg back in the frame and lay the second one in position across it so that they form an X into all four corners. With the upper piece held firmly, mark its position across the lower one. This will give you the angle at which to cut in fitting them together. Next, turn the legs over and mark the second one from the first. With your marking gauge, set off the depth of the cut (half the thickness of the wood) along the two sides of each piece. The cut is made by sawing inside the face lines of each leg and removing the waste with a chisel. Making

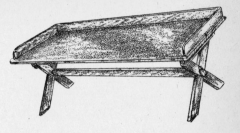

several parallel saw cuts to the exact depth facilitates this final operation.

When all four legs are made, and each pair fits together tightly, make sure both sets of legs are of the same height and stand perfectly straight. Then mark each pair so that the proper ones go together again. Now you are ready to cut the mortises for the stretcher, but do not do this until the stretcher tenons are finished. This operation is described later.

For the stretcher, plane material smooth to finished dimensions, and mark off tenon on each end (shoulder is 4⅜" from end and tenon 1¼" wide, 1½" high). Vertically through each tenon cut slot ½" wide, 1¼" long, with drill and chisel. This should extend from 1¼" from tenon shoulder to 1⅞" from the end.

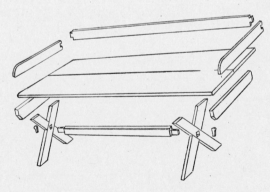

To fit stretcher slots, make two tapered pegs, 3″ high, ½″ thick, 1½″ wide at top (grain running vertically), and taper the front edge to ¾″ at bottom. Sand smooth to shape as shown after making guide saw cut under head.

Now assemble each pair of legs and mark them for tenon slots by drawing straight lines, one vertical, one horizontal, between the opposite angles, as shown. This gives a pair of center lines as guides for laying out the mortise. On these mark the hole

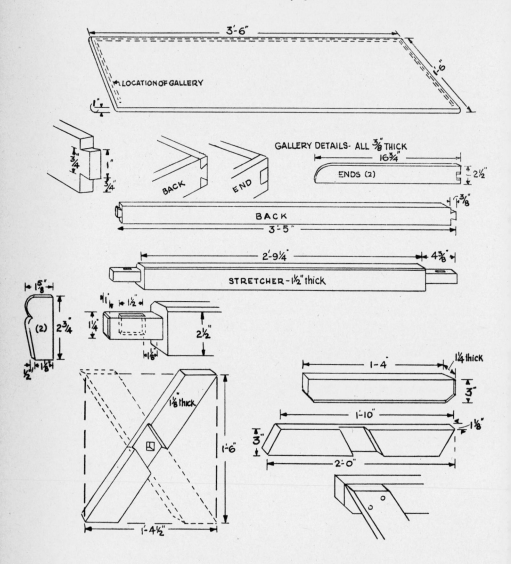

outline, 1" wide, 1½" high, and check this against the end of the tenon. Cut the mortise with the legs clamped together in position, first by drilling with a ⅞" bit, then finishing the squared sides with a chisel. Try the tenons for fit. Note that these holes must be exactly perpendicular to the face of the leg and vertical, otherwise the two pairs of legs will not be parallel with one another or to the floor.

Cut cleats to length; cut off lower corners at each end; chamfer lower and end edges on the outer side only; sand the end grain smooth and remove all sharp edges (arrises). About three inches from each end drill a ⅛" hole through the side and countersink. About 2½" from each end counterbore to a depth of 1", then drill through a hole (⅛" diameter) vertically, for attachment of table top.

Glue the leg half-lap joints, assemble, and clamp clear of holes (stretcher mortises). Insert tenons of stretcher in holes, then tap in pegs, lightly but firmly. Next fasten cleats to tops of legs with a No. 9 x 2" screw through each hole, after gluing faces. Now attach the whole leg assembly to the top. Do not glue cleats to top—the wide board must be allowed to expand and contract slightly, otherwise it will split. Use 1½" No. 9 screws for this. Check completed table on flat surface, and trim legs even, if necessary, by sanding bottoms. Finally, attach gallery by drilling three holes for the back and two for each side near their ends. These holes go through the table top and are countersunk on the underside. Glue gallery dovetails and assemble; glue bottom edges and clamp in position on the table top.

Turn table over and insert screws. Give whole t ble a final smooth sanding with .004 garnet paper. For finishes see Chapter VI.

LAMP TABLE

Wood: Pine throughout.

Material Requirements:

> Top—One piece ¾" x 17" x 18' (or two narrower
> pieces jointed and glued together as described in
> Chapter IV).
> Apron—Three pieces ⅞" x 5" x 14".
> Drawer Rails—Two pieces ¾" x 1½" x 14".
> Drawer Slides—Two pieces ⅝" x 1½" x 12"; two
> pieces ⅝" x ¾" x 13".
> Legs—Four pieces 1½" x 1½" x 28".
> Drawer (Front) One piece ¾" x 3½" x 12"; (back) one
> piece ½" x 3" x 12" (set ⅛" lower than sides);
> (sides) two pieces ½" x 3½' x 13⅜"; (bottom) one
> piece ³⁄₁₆" ply, or ¼" wood (bass or pine) (tapered
> at edges) 11⅜" x 13⅜".

Procedure:

Make top by cutting single piece to size, or jointing two pieces with glued butt joint, clamped. Tweny-four hours later trim to size, plane smooth on face, sand, taking off all top edge arrises (not the lower ones).

Mark off legs, leaving top 5" parallel sided 1½" square. Taper legs on two adjacent sides only, from the 5" line to bottom, making foot 1" square. With hand tools each leg will need to be tapered by rough sawing and planing to lines. With a bench saw you can make a guide strip as described in Chapter XI, tacking it to each leg in turn. In all cases see that the tapered sides are inside—i.e., that they do not form the outside corners of the table apron. Note that the tapered sides are the ones to be mortised for aprons and drawer rails, but do not make mortises till tenons are cut.

Cut apron to size and form tenons as shown. Note that when assembled the apron pieces are almost level with the outer faces of the legs, i.e., they are set in not more than ¹⁄₁₆". Drill for top screws down from the upper edges at a slight angle toward the inner face, then recess for the screw heads by making pockets on the inner face with a gouge.

Note that drawer top rail is dovetailed into tops of two front legs. Make these before recessing tops of legs. Drawer bottom rails are tenoned into legs.

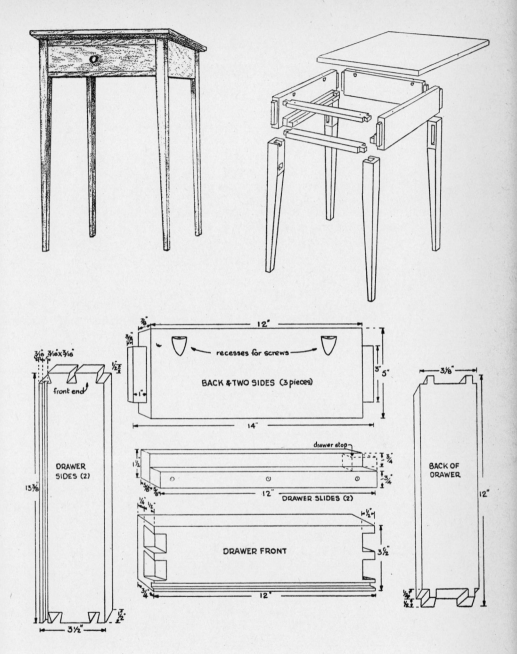

recesses for screws

BACK & TWO SIDES (3 pieces)

DRAWER SIDES (2)

front end

DRAWER SLIDES (2)

drawer stop

DRAWER FRONT

BACK OF DRAWER

Dimensions between shoulders of upper and lower rails must exactly match otherwise legs will not be parallel. With apron and rail pieces finished, cut legs to receive them. Assemble front first, then back and check one against the other for width and squareness. Then assemble side aprons, and, when clamped, see that all four legs are parallel along their outer faces. Disassemble, glue, and re-clamp. Before applying top, fit the drawer slides.

The drawer guides must fill in the difference between the thickness of the aprons and the thickness of the legs after assembly. Check guides for length in this space before gluing the drawer slides (runners) to them. They must be exactly parallel throughout their length or the drawer will not slide evenly. The slides must be glued to the guides before installation, and the slides must extend beyond the rear ends of the guides by a distance equal to the thickness of a guide. The slide will then fit snugly into the corner formed by the leg and

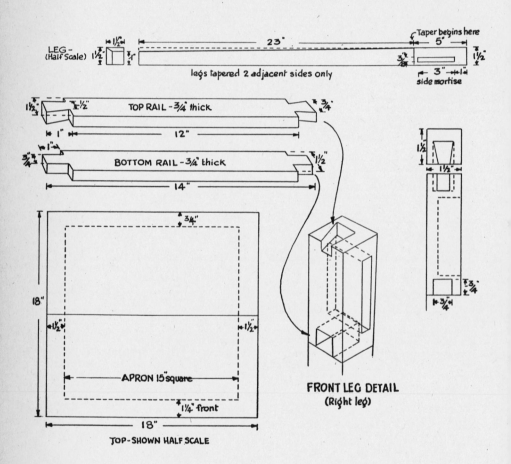

LEG — (Half Scale)

legs tapered 2 adjacent sides only

Taper begins here

side mortise

TOP RAIL — 3/4" thick

BOTTOM RAIL — 3/4" thick

18"

APRON 15" square

1 1/4" front

18"

TOP — SHOWN HALF SCALE

FRONT LEG DETAIL
(Right leg)

apron. The slide-guide assemblies can be screwed and glued to the aprons, taking care that they are exactly parallel with the bottom edges of the side aprons. With these small drawers it is not ordinarily necessary to fit a guide or kicker over the top edges of the drawer sides to prevent the drawer tipping when opened. However there is no objection to this extra refinement.

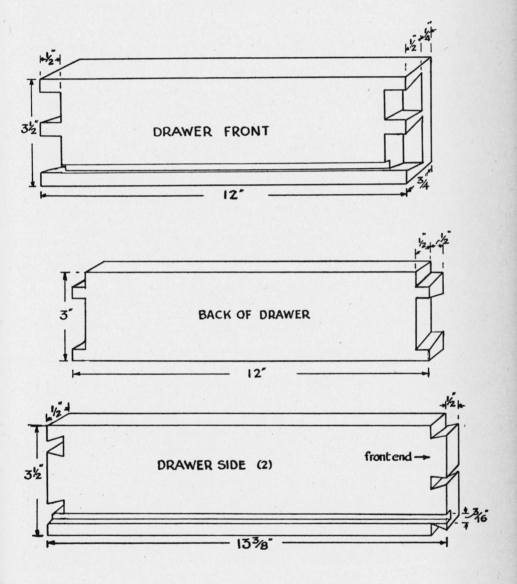

Mark out and fit the front of the drawer first, leaving the board ¹⁄₁₆" or more longer and wider than the opening. Finish the bottom and left-hand edge and fit them into the left-hand end of the opening. Next plane down the right-hand edge to fit the drawer front for length. Use a block against the end grain in planing, or chisel off the top corners to the thickness of the excess wood, to avoid splitting off the corner. Plane down the top edge to fit the opening vertically.

The drawer back is made next, ³⁄₈" shallower than the front and sides so as to clear the bottom board. It is also advisable to take off another ⅛" from the top so that it does not come as high as the sides. The back is fitted in practically the same manner as the front for length.

Rought-cut the drawer sides, planing bottom edge true and making front edge exactly at right angles to it. Check the two sides against one another for size and squareness. If there is a kicker, slide the sides in the drawer opening their full length as a check, and relieve any binding. The parts are now ready for dovetailing together, and the first step is to mark out all dimensions with a gauge. The dovetails on the sides are cut first, taking care to see that the groove for the drawer bottom is contained in the bottom tail. If the groove is too low, the groove in the back of the drawer front will show at the ends after assembly. Cut the sides of the tails with a saw (you can do both sides at once) and finish with a chisel exactly to the line. Do both ends of the sides, noting that the bottom pin of the back comes above the groove for the drawer bottom.

The drawer front is ¾" thick, and the dovetails are only ½" long, leaving a ¼" lap covering the tail ends. With the front held in a vise, hold the end of one side to the ¼" line and mark off the pins. Cut the sides of the pins as far as possible with a dovetail saw, and finish with a sharp chisel, checking the tail against the pins as the final trim paring cuts are made. In assembling the dovetails, hold the front firmly in a vise and drive in the tails by placing a block of wood over them and tapping gently. Do not hit the tails with a hammer. Cut the bottom groove in front and sides, and see that they come together exactly. Apply glue between the pins on final assembly.

The bottom is cut to exact size and perfectly square, then the front and side edges are eased slightly by sanding so that it will slide easily in the grooves. A solid wood bottom is usually made thicker than the plywood one, and the front and side edges tapered back for an inch or so. If the bottom is a good fit it should hold the drawer square while the glue sets. Check this with a square. Twenty-four hours later try the drawer in the table, and, if tight, ease the sides with a plane. In planing, support the drawer firmly so that it will not be forced out of square. A pair of 3" x 1" arms screwed to the bench top so that they project the depth of the drawer and hold it front and back will serve this purpose. Do not lubricate the sides or runners of the drawer until it has been fitted perfectly. Later the surfaces may be rubbed with paraffin wax. Small blocks can be glued to the rear of the runners to stop ths drawer entering beyond the point at which the front is perfectly level with the top and bottom rails (approximately ¹⁄₁₆" inside the front faces of the legs).

After the drawer work is completed, the top of the stand may be attached by screwing from the underside, but see that the overlap is reduced to ¾" at the back, with the front and sides overlapping the legs 1½" each way.

TRESTLE DINING TABLE

Wood: Pine or maple.

Material Requirements:

> Top—Sufficient pieces to make a board 60" long, 33"
> wide, smoothed, squared, and glue-jointed together
> as described in Chapter IV.
> Cleats—Two pieces 2" x 3½" x 30".
> Legs—Two pieces 1¾" x 8" x 29".
> Feet—Two pieces 3½" x 6" x 30".
> Stretcher—One piece 1½" x 4" x 51".
> Pegs—Two pieces ½" x 1½' x 4½".

Procedure:

Make top by cutting boards to length, planing smooth on face and edges; square and fit edges that are to form joints; glue and clamp. Twenty-four hours later scrape excess glue off face joints and ends; sand ends smooth and even, removing all sharp arrises and corners.

Cut cleats to size and plane smooth; cut corners at 45 degrees to half height of wood. Find the vertical center (15" from each end) and mark out slot 4" on each side to receive 8" leg. With marking gauge, set off depth of cut for legs to half thickness of cleat. Saw sides of slot to this depth, and a scant 8" wide. Make several saw cuts in between, the exact depth. Remove waste with chisel.

Drill one counterbored hole near each end of cleat (in tapered portion) for a 1½" x No. 9 screw. Chamfer off end and lower edges on outer side of each cleat. Sand edges and angles smooth.

Cut legs to exact length and plane smooth. Use cleat to mark off depth of rabbet at top of leg. With gauge, mark off depth of rabbet. Cut rabbet by sawing both across and along grain. Check by fitting cleat dado to the leg rabbet, and see that cleat is at exact right angles to the leg. Now cut tenon at opposite end of leg. The shoulder must be exactly 25½" from the top of the leg, and the tenon exactly 3½" long. Legs must match one another.

Cut feet to size, paying particular attention to thickness (vertically) so leg assemblies will be of exactly equal length. Mark out and saw tapered feet, trimming with chisel if necessary, and sand smooth. Mark out mortise, 4" x 1¼", and check against tenon. Cut mortise inside lines for tight fit.

Cut stretcher to size and plane smooth. Mark off top and bottom for end tenons. Note these are not shouldered at sides. Use marking gauge for longitudinal lines. Cut with saw, top and bottom, and saw down end grain, then smooth by sanding. Top edges can now be chamfered. Next, mark out the mortises on the legs, using the tenons as a guide to size after marking centers on legs. Check one

leg against the other to make sure centers are equidistant from ends. Cut leg mortises and fit tenons. These can be a sliding fit. With tenons pushed through mortises right up to their shoulders, pencil-mark them at the outer face of the legs as a guide and check for the peg holes to be made through the tenons. Remove the stretcher and mark out peg holes, starting about ⅛" behind pencil mark so that pegs will draw them tight. Finish holes smooth and square inside.

Cut two pegs out of pieces 1½" wide by 4" long. Mark down 1¼" from top and make shallow saw cut in one edge. This marks the end of the tapered part. Mark off 1" width at bottom of peg, and

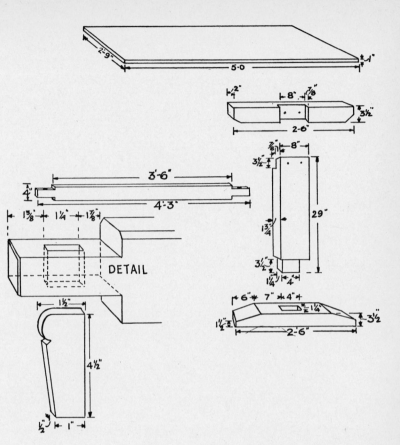

DETAIL

draw a line from this point to the notch for the taper cut. Round top by paring and sanding.

Assemble as follows: Glue leg tenon and tap gently into feet; checking angles with square in both directions. Attach battens with glue and two slightly counterbored 1½" x No. 9 screws. Plug with glued dowel stick sawn off level with surface. After glue is set, sand thoroughly all over, trimming plugs, if necessary, with sharp chisel first. Now assemble legs with stretcher and tap in peg firmly. Lay the table top, face down, on a clean floor, bench, or trestle, and place the leg assembly in position on it. The inside of each cleat should be 9 inches from the ends of the table top, but make them equal in any case. With the battens square with the edges of the top, clamp them in position with a stiff piece of lumber and a pair of C-clamps. Insert a 1½" x No. 9 screw in each hole and tighten it into the top. Do not use glue here. Plug the holes with dowel stick or wood paste and smooth them. Finally sand entire table, except under-surface of top, with fine garnet paper, 00 for maple and 0 for pine.

DROP-LEAF TABLE

Wood: Pine throughout, or pine top, maple legs and apron.

Material Requirements:

> Top—Six lengths ⅞" thick, 54" long, to make 1 top
> 18" wide, and 2 leaves 14" wide.
> Apron—Two pieces ¾" x 6" x 48", two pieces ¾" x
> 6" x 15".
> Legs—Four pieces 2" x 2" x 29".
> Leaf Brackets—Two pieces ¾" x 3" x 20¾".
> Hinges—Six butt type, 1½" x 1½".
> Dowels—Nine ½" x 2".
> Bracket Pivots—Four 10d nails, heads cut off.
> Screws—Thirty-six ¾" x No. 9 countersink.

Procedure:

Make top and leaves from three pairs of boards, making square joint edges, and matching each pair till no light shows between edges (see Chapter IV). Join edges with three dowels, one in center and one 3" from each end of boards. Mark dowel center lines while boards are together. Separate boards and carry center lines across edges. Mark centers of lines with gauge, and drive a ¾" finishing nail in halfway and cut off heads. Lay boards on a perfectly flat surface and press edges together (the board ends being in line) so nails in one mark centers in other. Remove nails and use holes as centers in drilling holes (1⅛" deep) for dowels. Cut dowels 2" long, groove and glue (as described in Chapter VI) and drive into one hole. Glue edges of

both boards and lay on flat surface with dowels opposite holes in other board. Apply clamps to draw two boards together. Leave clamped and set aside to dry. Twenty-four hours later cut boards to approximate finished dimensions and smooth face side. Carefully match all three pieces for length.

To make legs, mark outside adjoining faces (for identification) and taper inside adjoining faces, starting 6" down from top. Tops of legs, for first 6" should be 2" square; the feet 1¼" square (see note pp. 101-105). Mark top ends of tapered sides for mortises, but do not outline mortises till apron tenons are made.

Cut apron boards to exact length, then mark off tenons, all of which are 3" long. Find vertical

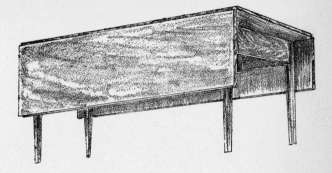

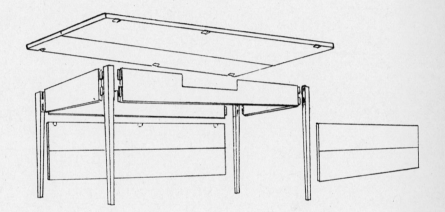

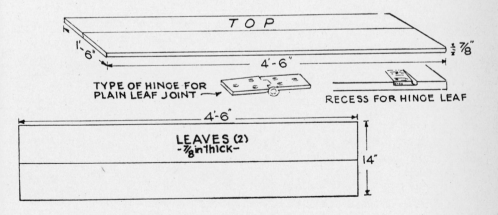

TOP

1'-6"

4'-6"

½ 7/8"

TYPE OF HINGE FOR
PLAIN LEAF JOINT →

RECESS FOR HINGE LEAF

4'-6"

LEAVES (2)
-7/8 in thick-

14"

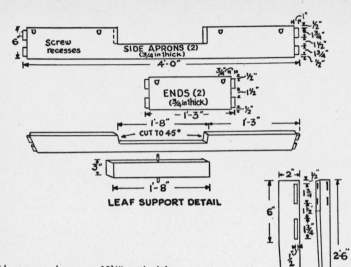

LEAF SUPPORT DETAIL

LEGS (4)
Tapered 2 inside faces only

center of side apron and measure 10⅜" on the left side of it and 9⅝" on the other side of it. Bring these lines down 3" on the apron face so that you have a rectangle 3" x 20". Set bevel protractor to 45 degrees and mark off the saw cut on the top edge of apron from the two vertical lines. Both of these bevel lines run from left to right with respect to the outer face of the apron so that you have a 20" opening cut at 45 degrees through the wood.

Instead of making a single wide tenon at each end of the four apron pieces, two narrower ones are used to give greater joint strength. The tenons are made ½" thick and 1¾" wide, with a space of 1½" between them. In squaring top and bottom edges of these boards you can also drill down at a slight angle through the edges for screws to hold the top. Then form pockets for the screw heads with a gouge. The next operation is to mark off the mortises on the legs from the tenons. A sharp point should be used for this to ensure tight fit. The mortises can be roughly drilled out with a ⅜" bit to a depth of ¾" and finished with a ½" chisel. The outer edge of the mortise should be no more than 3⁄16" from the outer face of the leg, so great

care must be exercised to drill and cut exactly at right angles to the leg surface.

With all mortises cut, the aprons and legs can be assembled, joints being glued and the whole tightly clamped and checked for squareness. Greater rigidity can be secured by tacking two laths diagonally across the tops of the legs. While the glue is setting, the leaf brackets can be made, and the pivot nails driven into holes drilled in the top and bottom edges at the center. The lower nails are cut off at the head, leaving about 1½" in the bracket, and 1½" to go into holes in the apron. The upper nails are cut shorter so that they enter the table top no more than ⅝". Placing the bracket in position in the apron slot, and tapping the upper hinge nail sharply will mark the apron where the hole must be drilled for the bottom pin. The top hole is located by clamping the bracket in the closed position and placing the whole base assembly upside down on the table top which has been laid face down on the bench or floor. First, however, the underside of the top should be carefully marked in indicate the exact position of the four legs. The top overlap beyond the legs is 3" at each end, and only ¼" at the sides.

After the pin holes have been drilled in the top, the top and leaves should be assembled. The top and one leaf are first laid on a flat surface, and the ends lined up exactly. The hinges are then opened and laid in position. A line is scratched around each one, and cuts are made, as shown, to sink the hinge and its pin into the thickness. The center knuckle of the hinge should be exactly in line with the joint, and the joint should be kept tightly closed when marking centers for the screws. With this type of joint the hinge knuckle will show when the leaf hangs, but the gap can be kept small by careful fitting. The hinges are firmly screwed to the table top before the top is attached to the base. Finally, the leaves are attached while the table is laid flat on its face.

HUTCH TABLE

Wood: Pine or oak.

Material Requirements:

> Top—Five pieces 1″ x 8½″ x 42″ t&g, or equivalent, to make 42″ dia.
> circular top.
> Base Sides—Two pieces 1″ x 14″ x 27½″.
> Base Front and Back—Two pieces 1″ x 12″ x 18″.
> Lid—Two pieces t&g to make 14″ x 16½″.
> Lid Battens—Two pieces ¾″ x 2″ x 12″.
> Seat Bottom—Two pieces ¾″ t&g to make 12″ x 16½″.
> Cleats—Two pieces ¾″ x ¾″ x 12″, two pieces ¾″ x ¾″ x 16½″.
> Feet—Two pieces 2½″ x 2½″ x 19″, one piece ¾″ x 4″ x 16½′.
> Pins—Four pieces of 1″ dowel x 3½″; 30″ of ½″ dowel for top pegs, if
> used in place of screws.

Procedure:

Cut 5 or more lengths of t&g board to total 42″ wide, as shown, from which a circle 42″ diameter can be cut. Glue and clamp together; leave 24 hours to set. Select a point as center and drive in part way a small finishing nail. With a cord attached to the nail, and a pencil or chalk at a distance of 21″, describe the circle. (A thin lath with V-notches at each end can be used instead of the string.) Saw to the line and finish with a rasp and sanding. Usually it is preferable to work on the top after the cleats have been attached. Plane face flat and smooth.

Cut battens from square with a scroll saw after marking out on both faces. This is properly a job

for a power jig saw or a ⅛″ band saw. Finish edge by sanding. Mark center lines for 1″ pegs that hold the top to the base 5½″ either side the center line. The battens are mounted on the underside of the top, each 10″ from the extreme edge. If the battens are 2″ thick they will be 18″ apart and fit snugly over the base. Battens are fastened to top either by screws, counterbored and having the holes plugged with dowel stick, or with glued pegs. If pegs are used, the holes are drilled right through the batten and the top. Pegs must be tight fit and the battens must not be glued to the top or contraction and expansion may split the boards. Be sure the 1″ peg holes holding the top to the base are drilled before the battens are attached; afterward it will be most difficult.

For the base proceed as follows: Cut the 1" x 14" x 31½" ends to shape, but do not start the dovetail joints. The decorative curves are best made freehand, but a cut-out of plywood or even paper will help get all four alike. The first step is to mark off 2½" from the bottom of the sides for tenons. The finished seat will be 23½" from the bottom. The lid being 1" thick the top of the back and front dovetailed pieces is 22½" high. This corresponds to 5½" from the top. Mark each edge at this point,

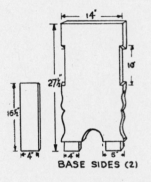

BASE SIDES (2)

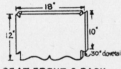

SEAT FRONT & BACK

DETAIL OF FOOT

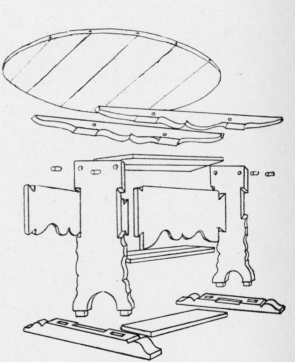

LAYING OUT TABLE TOP ON OAK BOARDS

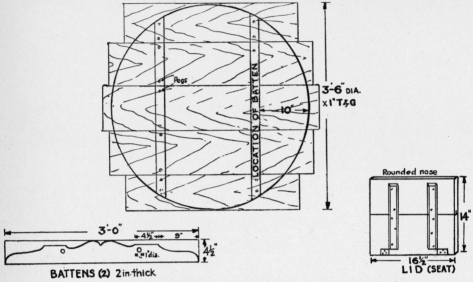

3'-6" DIA.
X 1" T & G

Pegs

LOCATION OF BATTEN

10"

Rounded nose

14"

16½"
LID (SEAT)

3'-0"

4½"   9"

4½"

o   1'dia.

BATTENS (2) 2 in. thick

then measure a further 10" down for the bottom of the dovetail. Note that the seat front and back are 2" wider than the dovetail. Therefore the edges of the end pieces should be straight and square for 2" below the dovetail. Mark this point, then divide the remaining length to the tenons in two, and mark the center where the two double curves meet. This center line will be 6¼" from the bottom, and each double curve will be 3¾" long. The curve should not extend inward more than the depth of the dovetail, i.e., 1".

Above the bottom line marking depth of tenons is a 4" semicircle. It is generally better to cut this after the tenons are made. The tenons have a ½" shoulder each end, and only a 3/16" shoulder at the sides. The tenons therefore are 5/8" thick. Cut these next. The peg holes at the top are best centered by holding one of them against the top

battens and poking the 1" drill through the batten peg holes.

Place both end pieces in a vise together and drill right through, taking care that the drill is exactly at right angles to the wood.

Next make the front and back pieces. Cut the tails and use them to mark out the cuts on the end pieces. The ends of the front and back pieces must be exactly square, and so must the dovetail shoulders. The curves are cut as before.

The best method of supporting the bottom of the seat is to screw and glue ¾" x ¾" strips all around the inside of the front, side, and back pieces. These must be set up high enough (1") so as not to show below the side curves. The two pieces of ¾" board that form the bottom do not need to be fastened together before being set in place. They are carefully fitted and supported on the ¾" fillets. The holding screws are then inserted through the fillets from underneath.

With the box part assembled, and all checked for squareness, the feet are added. The mortises are marked from the tenons, and the lamb's tongue ends spaced off and marked for cutting. When the mortises are cut, right through the feet, the feet are fitted temporarily. The 4" tie board or stretcher, cut to length and squared, is placed in position, and the slots to receive it marked out on both feet, for depth as well as length and width. The feet are then removed and the dadoes cut. The stretcher ends are glued and fastened in position with short countersunk screws. The feet are put back on the tenons which have been glued. These should be a tight fit, otherwise thin wedges will have to be driven in from the underside to anchor them.

The last operation is the fitting of the lid, the top edge of the back being recessed for the hinges. This needs no explanation.

MODERN TRAY TABLE

Wood: Maple and plywood.

Material Requirements:

> Bottom—One piece ½" ply, 20" x 32".
> Gallery—Two pieces 4" x 36", two pieces 4" x 24"
> (½" maple).
> Moulding—Half-round, 10 ft. of ⅜"; quarter-round,
> 9 ft. of ½".
> Base—One piece ½" ply, 18½" x 20".
> Legs—Four pieces 2" x 2" x 19" (maple).
> Handles—One piece 1" x 3½ x 6" (maple); four ¾"
> x No. 10 c.s. screws.
> Twelve 2" x No. 12 c.s. screws.

Procedure:

Cut out bottom plywood to finished dimensions; this will serve as a guide for other pieces. Cut the four L-shaped pieces to form base, but do not cut mortises till the leg tenons are made. These four pieces, when assembled, should fit sides of bottom exactly. Now make legs, with the grain as nearly parallel to the sides as possible; form the tenons on top, and see that the legs are of exactly equal length, and the tenons at right-angles to the upper face. In laying out these legs it pays to make a jig by tacking four pieces of lath to the bench top, forming an accurate rectangle as indicated in the leg drawing. Working from a length of 2" x 2" stock, the foot and top are cut to the proper angle

first. With the 2" x 2" inside the jig, the shoulder also is marked off on two opposite sides. Then mark and cut the taper on the two inside faces only. Finally, make the tenon. With the legs finished, cut the mortise and attach the legs with glue and finishing nails. See that the tenon ends are perfectly flush with the faces of the plywood pieces. Now assemble base and bottom.

With the bottom face down, place the leg and base assemblies in position on it. After checking for fit, glue the faces of the four base pieces and clamp them in position on the bottom board. Leave to set while making the tray sides or gallery.

The sides are all of ½" stock. Cut ends to 60

degrees as shown, and plane bottom and top edges to 30 degrees. Join all mitered corners with glue and 1½" finishing nails. Invert the gallery on a flat board or bench top and hold square with clamps

till glue is set. Then check evenness of lower edges by standing the gallery in final position on the bottom board. Trim high spots by sanding. Mount on bottom by laying the gallery on a flat surface, upside down, and turning base assembly over on it. The edges of the gallery should be glued and the base clamped to it, still upside down. Now drill 12 holes, as indicated, through the base and bottom into the rim, all at an angle of 60 degrees, with

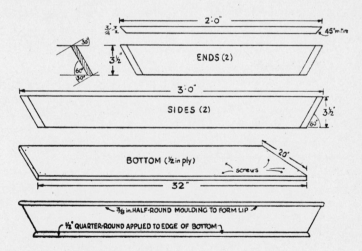

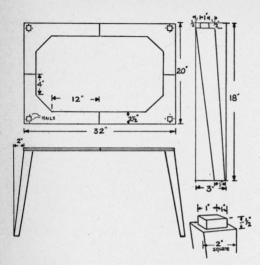

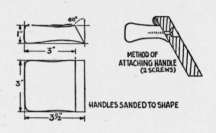

METHOD OF
ATTACHING HANDLE
(2 SCREWS)

HANDLES SANDED TO SHAPE

centers ¼" from the base edge. These holes should enter the gallery parallel to its sides for about ¾". Insert 2" No. 12 or No. 10 c.s. screws and tighten.

To finish, lightly plane or sand top edges of gallery till they are quite straight and in line. Then miter finish mouldings and apply them with glue and 1" finishing nails. Note that the quarter-round moulding goes on the edge of the bottom, forming a flange that practically hides the edges of the base plywood.

The handles are installed last, and the screw counterbores plugged with surface-grain wood that should be matched up as carefully as possible so that they will not show when finished.

JOINT STOOL

Wood: Pine or walnut.

Material Requirements:

> Top—One piece 1¼" x 16" x 16".
> Apron—Four pieces ¾" x 7½" x 13½".
> Legs—Four pieces 1½" x 1½" x 27".
> Stretchers—Four pieces 1¼" x 1½" x 13½".
> Screws—Eight 1½" No. 9 c.s.

Procedure:

Use squared paper to make a pattern for cut-out portion of four aprons. Square and smooth four apron boards to finished size. Mark off tenons with line around, ¾" from end. Trace pattern and cut out with coping saw or jig saw. Finish cut edges with sandpaper and remove all sharp arrises. Cut out tenons, ⅜" thick.

Next make legs. These finish to 1½" square, but they are more easily cut with a saw if you use 2" stock. This enables you to saw (preferably with a band saw) with the tool in the wood from one end to the other. Each of the four sides must be shaped, but it is easier to judge symmetry if opposite sides are done first, i.e., sides 1 and 3, then 2 and 4. Done by hand, the simplest procedure is to make a saw cut all around at the top and bottom of the tapered portion. Depth of saw cut will be a scant ¼" if the stock is 1½" square, and the excess will have to be pared away with a chisel. The rounding can be roughed out with a fine rasp and finished with sandpaper. Keep the arrises fairly sharp. The mortises are marked out close to the front faces of the legs, but leave stock not less than 3/16" thick for strength. In the case of these aprons the thickness can very well be ¼".

The feet of the legs are almost round, and are cut from the square first into octagons after making a fine saw cut at shoulder depth. The corners can then be rasped and sanded off.

The stretchers are made heavy to withstand rough

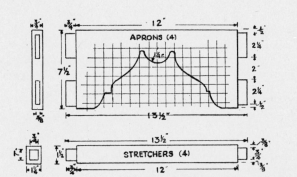

APRONS (4)

STRETCHERS (4)

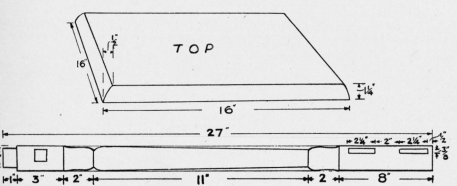

TOP

usage and allow for excessive wear, and the tenons are made much thicker than usual. Although the tenons are only ¾" long they should be firm if properly glued and clamped, but there is no objection to driving a finishing nail from the back. A somewhat decorative alternative would be to insert thin pegs of hardwood, allowing the heads to project ⅛". This adds to the antique air of the piece besides positively locking the joint.

Finally, the top is made. It should preferably be of one piece and have an interesting grain.

There is no bead, but the edges are rounded off to the depth of the overhang. The top is secured to the aprons by means of two screws in each, with pockets, for the heads.

The holes are drilled down through the edge of the apron pieces at an angle, and the pocket then gouged out (on the inside of the apron) before the parts are assembled.

A common alternative is to apply ¾" x ¾" strips to the inside tops of the aprons, after assembly, and screw into the top board through these.

LOOSE-SEAT STOOL

Wood: Pine or maple.

Material Requirements:

Legs—Four pieces 1½" x 1½" x 10".
Rails—Two pieces 1¼" x 2" x 14', two pieces 1¼" x
2" x 11".
Stretchers—Two pieces 1" x 1¼" x 10½", one piece
1" x 1¼" x 13½".
Corner Blocks—Four pieces ¾" x 3½" x 3½".
Loose-Seat Rails—Two pieces ⅞" x 2½" x 14".
Dowels—Four pieces ⅜" x 2", four pieces ⅜' x 1¼".

Procedure:

Make legs from dimensioned and planed lengths and mark out for rails and stretcher tenons. Note that rail tenons are shouldered half their length, and set down ¾" from top of the leg to allow for the rail rabbet which is extended into the top of the leg. The mortise is best cut before the top of the leg is recessed. The mortises are cut deep so that one enters the other and some extra tenon length is secured by mitering the tenon ends. All of this calls for careful fitting. The stretcher mortises are centered in the face of the leg so that the stretchers are set in ¼" from the sides of the leg. In these cases it is best to make the tenoned parts first and match them up. Then, if there is a slight error in

dimensioning the actual tenons, adjustments can be made in the mortises.

The rail tenon is ½" from the outer face so that the rail inner face is ¼" from the inner face of the leg.

This makes it necessary to cut a ¼" x ¼" notch in the corner blocks, actually a shade more, to clear the leg arris and make certain the block faces are tight against the rails. Incidentally, do not glue the blocks when you install them or they cannot be tightened later.

In recessing the tops of the legs, saw to both side and bottom lines as far as possible and finish with a very sharp chisel. Shoulders of rails must fit

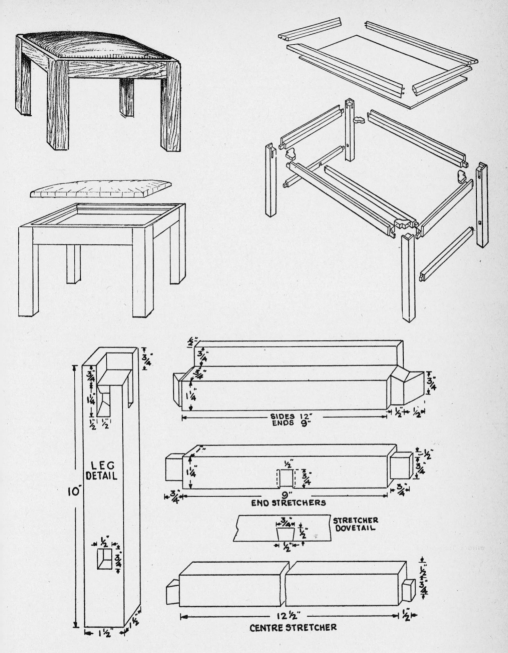

LEG
DETAIL

10"

SIDES 12"
ENDS 9"

9"
END STRETCHERS

STRETCHER
DOVETAIL

12½"
CENTRE STRETCHER

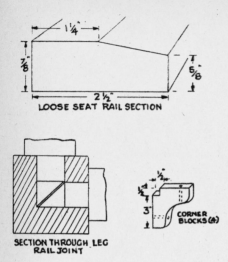

LOOSE SEAT RAIL SECTION

SECTION THROUGH LEG
RAIL JOINT

CORNER
BLOCKS (4)

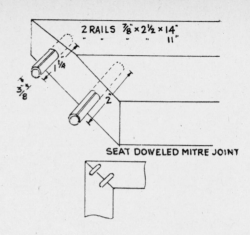

SEAT DOWELED MITRE JOINT

tight against the leg shoulders so that no joint is visible after gluing and clamping.

In making the stretcher, complete all cutting and fitting to exact dimensions before assembling in the legs, and check after temporary assembly. The dovetails of the cross-stretcher should fit tightly. The length between the shoulders must be exact or the side stretchers will be bowed, either in or out. After

careful fitting of all base units, glue and clamp and, after 24 hours, apply the corner blocks.

The removable seat consists of a simple $\frac{7}{8}$" x $2\frac{1}{2}$" frame with mitered and doweled corners. The inner half of the top is beveled so that no sharp edge cuts into the webbing and no ridge is formed that will show through the upholstery. This can be finished in any way desired, using rubber or hair and cotton for the seat. The amount of clearance to be left around the frame will depend on the upholstery details.

FIVE-BOARD BENCH

Wood: Pine.

Material Requirements:

> Top—One piece ⅞" x 8¾" x 18".
> Apron—Two pieces ¾" x 5" x 14".
> Legs—Two pieces ¾" x 9' x 14½'.
> Drawer—(Front) one piece ¾" x 3" x 8"; (sides) two
> pieces ¼" x 2" x 6¼"; (back) one piece ⁵⁄₁₆" x 1⅜'
> x 7"; (bottom) one piece ¼" x 5¾" x 6".
> Cleats and drawer slides and guides cut to measure.

Procedure:

Cut the two legs to size from a 9" board, and taper each side ½" toward the top. Cut in shoulders for the aprons 5" from the top to ¾" deep on either side. Mark the center of the board 4½" to 5" from the bottom. From this point draw a double curve, as shown, to make a pair of feet 2" wide. If this proves difficult, make a paper pattern first. Next make the two aprons, if necessary using a paper pattern drawn on 1" squares. Cut out drawer opening on front apron so that top and bottom lips will be parallel with floor when assembled.

Assemble legs and aprons with clamps so that legs are about 3" farther apart at bottom than at top. Mark this position on the inside of the aprons,

both sides of the leg. Before attaching the cleats, drill holes for two screws through the ¾" thickness to take the screws that hold the leg. Glue and screw cleats to aprons. Lay each leg in position against the apron and mark the waste to be cut away in fitting the apron to the shoulder. Trim this to shape before proceeding further. Glue and screw the cleats to the legs while the four pieces are clamped together. Since the legs are tilted, a corner will project above the apron. Pare this off with a chisel so that the top of the leg is even with the top edge of the apron. You will also need to take a shaving off the outside edge of each apron as these are also slightly tilted.

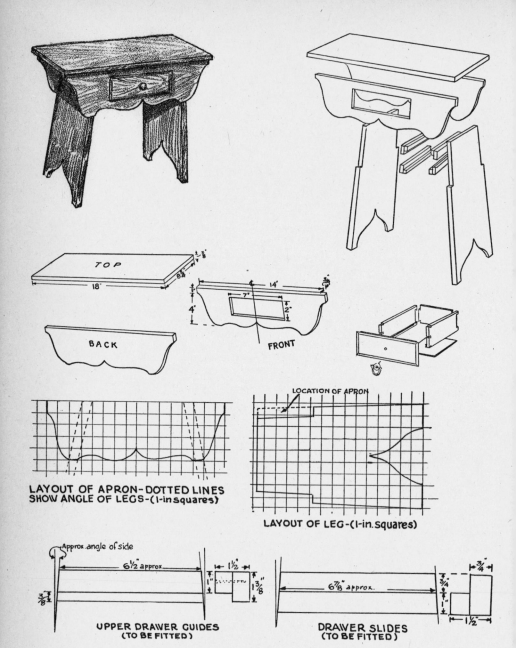

TOP

18"   8¼"   ⅛"

14"   ¾"

BACK

FRONT   7"   4"   2"

LOCATION OF APRON

**LAYOUT OF APRON-DOTTED LINES
SHOW ANGLE OF LEGS-(1-in squares)**

LAYOUT OF LEG-(1-in. Squares)

Approx. angle of side

6½" approx.   1½"   1"   3⅛"   ⅜"

**UPPER DRAWER GUIDES
(TO BE FITTED)**

6⅞" approx.   ¾"   ¾"   ½"   1½"

**DRAWER SLIDES
(TO BE FITTED)**

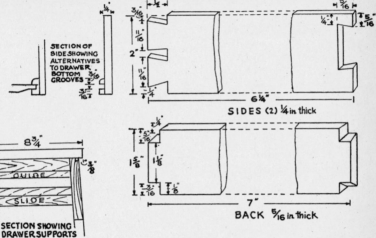

SIDES (2) ¼ in thick

BACK ⁵⁄₁₆ in thick

SECTION OF SIDE SHOWING ALTERNATIVES TO DRAWER BOTTOM GROOVES

SECTION SHOWING DRAWER SUPPORTS

Next cut and finish the top to size. Lay it in position on the aprons, projecting two inches at each end. On the underside of the top, mark the position of the top (outside) of each leg. Remove the top and screw another pair of cleats to it along this line, first making two more holes in each for the screws that go into the top ends of the legs. These cleats

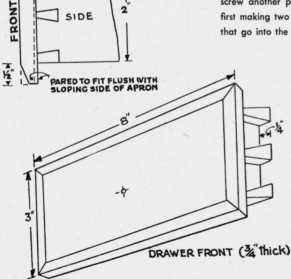

DRAWER FRONT (¾" thick)

will not be more than 6" long. After fitting top, with cleats attached, and seeing that it beds down evenly all around, set it aside and make the drawer runners and guides. These need to be carefully fitted to the slope of the aprons, using the corners of the drawer opening as guides.

The simplest and most substantial method of attachment is to build out the inner sides of the legs with triangular pieces and attach the runners to their faces. The same effect is secured by making the guides an inch or so thicker, and cutting them to shape as required. The whole unit is then glued and screwed to the legs. The same system is followed with the top guides. Carefully check the drawer guides and slides to see they are absolutely parallel. Then make the drawer.

The drawer is both shallow and short and should be made of wood as thin as possible. With thin sides it will not be possible to make dados for the bottom without unduly weakening them. Instead, glue a square strip along the inner bottom edge of each side, $\frac{1}{8}$" or $\frac{3}{16}$" thick. An eighth of an inch above this glue another strip which has its top outer corner rounded off. This will leave a $\frac{1}{8}$" groove for the bottom board to slide in. The front of the drawer, being sufficiently thick, can be grooved as usual. If the bottom is made of solid wood it should preferably be no less than $\frac{3}{16}$" to $\frac{1}{4}$" thick, with the front and two side edges tapered off to $\frac{1}{8}$" or less. The back of the drawer is cut narrower, as usual, to clear the bottom, which can be kept from sliding out by means of a small brad.

SIDE CHAIR AND ARM CHAIR

Wood: Maple.

Material Requirements:

> Legs—Two boards 1¼" x 5" x 36", two boards 1¼" x
> 2" x 17½".
> Rails—One piece 1½" x 2½" x 17, one piece 1½"
> x 2½" x 15", two pieces, 1½" x 2½" x 14½".
> Corner Blocks—Four pieces 1¼" x 4" x 7".
> Back Rails—Two pieces 1" x 1¼" x 15", one piece
> 1¼" x 1¼" x 16½".
> Slip-Seat—One piece ply, ¼" x 15" x 15"; four pieces
> pine or bass, ¾" x 2" x 15".

Procedure for Side Chair:

Cut out rear legs by sawing out of 5" x 36" plank, after marking out as shown in drawing. Sand back of center portion into smooth curve. Next mark out for four mortises and cut tenon on top; cut out front legs, tapered on two inside faces only. Mark out tops for seat recesses, each 1" deep, 1½" wide along front, and 1" along the side. Angle cuts are made with a saw and the job is finished with a very sharp chisel. The seat rails are cut next, and it is usually best to make the front and rear ones before cutting the side rails. As usual, the rails are rabbeted, then the tenons are formed. Next, the mortises for these tenons are cut in front and back legs. In each case the rails should be approximately flush with the outside surfaces of the legs. When rails and their joints have been properly made and checked for squareness, the more complicated side rails are made. The important job on the side rails is to mark out the shoulders at the correct angle. This is best done by first laying out the chair frame, full size, on a sheet of brown paper. The outlines of the side rails are then cut out to form a pattern, ignoring the tenons. The ends of the pattern will then form the proper angle and can be laid on the wood as a guide in marking.

The tenons are made at right angles to the shoulders and therefore at an angle to the sides of the rails. It is well to check one rail against the other to see that the pairs of angles are equal. When the tenons are finished they are used as

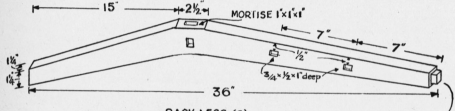

BACK LEGS (2)

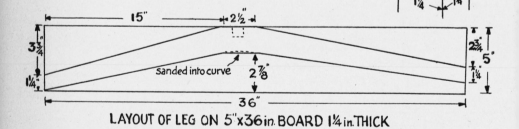

LAYOUT OF LEG ON 5"x36 in. BOARD 1¼ in. THICK

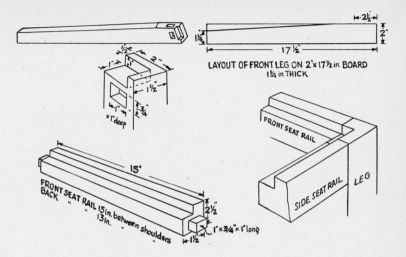

LAYOUT OF FRONT LEG ON 2"x 17½ in. BOARD
1¼ in. THICK

marking guides for their mortises, and the mortises are cut at right angles to the faces of the legs as usual.

The entire seat frame and legs can now be assembled, on a perfectly flat surface, for a final check on symmetry both horizontal and vertical. Following this, the two back rails and top rail are made. The two lower rails are carefully checked for length against the back seat rail and against one another. These rails serve more as a back rest than as a structural part of the chair. However, they should have the mortises cut, and should be assembled before fitting the top rail.

The top rail extends the full width of the back of the chair, i.e., the length of the seat rail, from shoulder to shoulder, plus the thickness of the two legs. The blind mortises are cut near each end so that they fit snugly over the tenons on the tops of the back legs. With the rail held firmly in this position by the tight tenons, the top corners are rounded off with a plane and the top and ends finished with sandpaper so that all faces are in line

with the legs and the joints barely visible. These tenons should be snugly fitted because only glue is relied upon to hold them.

If it is desired to upholster the back, canvas can be passed around top and bottom rails (or top and second rails) to hold a foam rubber pad and form a foundation for the surface upholstery material. When the whole chair is ready for final assembly, front and back joints are glued and put together first and firmly clamped. Then the side rails are added, and the seat of the frame squared up symmetrically and clamped.

At this point the corner blocks are prepared and inserted, being glued and screwed firmly in position. They need fitting carefully so as not to pull the seat out of shape. Sound pieces of sycamore or bass will serve for these. Finally, the seat cushion frame is made, taking the dimensions directly from the seat frame rabbet. Corners will need to be cut out for the rear legs, and the back strip must be amply wide to allow for this without excessively weakening the open mortise joints.

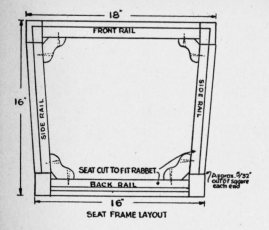

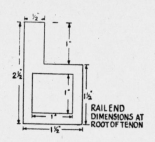

SEAT FRAME LAYOUT

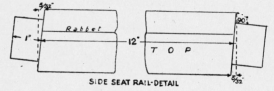

SIDE SEAT RAIL-DETAIL

Wood: Maple.

Material Requirements:

>Back Legs—Two pieces 1¼" x 5" x 36".
>Front Legs—Two pieces 1¼" x 2" x 27".
>Seat Rails—One piece 1½" x 2½" x 17"; one piece
>   1½" x 2½" x 15"; two pieces 1½" x 2½" x 14½".
>Corner Blocks—Four pieces 1¼" x 4" x 7'.
>Slip Seat—One piece ply ¼" x 15" x 15"; four pieces
>   pine or bass ¾" x 2" x 15".
>Back Rail—One piece 1" x 1¼" x 15".
>Arms—Two pieces 1½" x 1¾" x 17½".

Procedure for Arm Chair:

Procedure as for the side chair is followed, with some exceptions. There will be no rabbet in the front legs for the seat. Instead, the seat cushion frame is notched at the front corners. The arms are mortised before they are shaped so that you have a strong, solid and square piece to work on. The

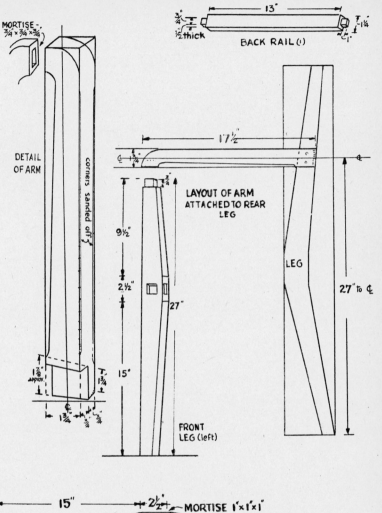

BACK RAIL (1)

DETAIL OF ARM

corners sanded off

MORTISE — 3/4 × 3/4 × 3/4

13"

1/2 thick

1 1/4

1"

LAYOUT OF ARM ATTACHED TO REAR LEG

17 1/2"

LEG

27" to ℄

9 1/2"

2 1/2"

27"

15"

1 3/8 approx.

1 3/4

1 3/4

3/4

3/4

FRONT LEG (left)

15"

2 1/2"

MORTISE 1"×1"×1"

9" ℄

B

1/2"

3/4 × 1/2 × 1" deep

1 1/4

1 1/4

36"

BACK LEG

angle of the rabbet, where the arm joins the back leg, is marked directly from the leg. Finally, the arm is shaped with a spokeshave followed by sanding after the deep cut on the underside has been roughly sawed and chiseled out. The back end of the arm is attached to the leg with two screws, slightly countersunk and their heads covered with a thin disc of wood, rounded on the surface to project slightly and simulate pegs.

The back of the arm chair can easily be upholstered in the same manner as the side chair, though the pad will be much shallower than the one covering three back rails.

WING CHAIR

Wood: Pine.

Material Requirements:

Wing and Side Units—Two pieces ¾″ x 12″ x 36″, two pieces ¾″ x 8″ x 12″, or equivalent (see text).

Arms—Two pieces ¾″ x 5″ x 17″, four pieces triangular or cove moulding, 1½″ x 1½′ x 16″.

Back—Three pieces ¾″ x 2½″ x 18½″, two pieces ¾″ x 2½″ x 35¼″.

Seat—Two pieces ¾″ x 2½″ x 24″, one piece ¾″ x 2½″ x 18¾″, one piece ¾″ x 2½″ x 20½″.

Upholstery Frame—(Back) Three pieces ⅝″ x 2½″ x 18″, two pieces ⅝″ x 2½″ x 33¼″; (seat) two pieces ⅝″ x 2½″ x 23¼″, one piece ⅝″ x 2½″ x 20″.

Legs—Two pieces 2″ x 2″ x 11″, two pieces 2″ x 3″ x 11″.

Rails—(Side) Two pieces 1½″ x 2″ x 22″; (front) one piece ½″ x 2″ x 20″; (rear) one piece 1½″ x 2″ x 18″.

Stretchers—Two pieces ¾″ x 1¼″ x 22″, one piece ¾″ x 1¼″ x 20½″.

Trim—Two pieces ⅝″ x 3″ x 25¼″, one piece ⅝″ x 3″ x 19¾″, one piece ⅝″ x 3″ x 23¼″.

Procedure:

In this piece the base is the governing unit and should be made first. The top part is then fitted to it and the dimensions adjusted accordingly, though they should vary but little. Note that the front legs are square and straight; the rear ones are curved backward to counteract the otherwise top-heavy appearance of the sloping back while increasing the stability. The back legs are cut from 2″ x 3″ material, and the sloping does not start at the top but 2″ down. This presents a square surface to the side frame member and makes fitting easier.

The four rails are heavy and strongly jointed, with haunched tenons to take full advantage of their depth. These tenons are marked as 1″ long but should be scant. The best way to cut these mortises is to drill the square part the full depth, and, when chiseling out, to cut the upper corner out only after most of the square portion has been cleared. The chisel must be very sharp so as not to split the wood due to working at an angle across the grain. If the tenons are made first they can be used to check the depth and shape of the mortise.

In making the side-rail joints, the shoulder cuts
are carefully marked at the proper angle. This
angle is best determined as described on pp. 99-
101 immediately preceding. The assembly is greatly
strengthened by an H-stretcher, tenoned into the
legs fore-and-aft, and tied together with a transverse piece dovetailed into them. These dovetails
need to be carefully made and close-fitting. The
tails are made first, four-fifths of the depth of the
side pieces. These joints must be a good fit and
strongly glued or the side members will be greatly
weakened. The side-piece tenons must allow for
the angle of the tenon shoulders (the same angle
as that of the side rails). The transverse stretcher
is best fitted last when the rest of the base, includ-

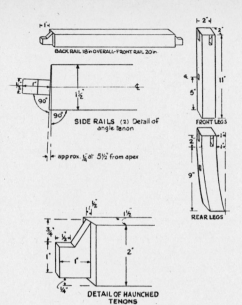

BACK RAIL 18 in OVERALL—FRONT RAIL 20 in.

SIDE RAILS (2) Detail of
angle tenon

approx. ⅛ at 5½ from apex

DETAIL OF HAUNCHED
TENONS

FRONT LEGS

REAR LEGS

ing the fore-and-aft stretchers, has been assembled,
glued, and clamped. If the dovetails are a good
press fit it will not need clamping.

The wings can be made next, and the first operation is to lay out the curved portion. It will be
necessary to make the wing side unit of two pieces,
srongly joined. Since the wing measures 12″ across
at its widest part, a board of that width is needed.
A full-size pattern of the shape should be made on
heavy paper, with 2″ squares. This is cut out and
laid on the 12″ board with the back line of the
pattern parallel with the back edge of the board.
This will show how much more is needed to complete the side, and the angle at which the joint will
have to be made. This joint should be a glued
tongue-and-groove because the side needs to be
supported its full height (8″).

Note that the grain of the wing unit runs vertically,
and the rest of the arm unit should do this also.
Since you presumably have a 12″ wide board, this
should present no difficulty. Otherwise, two nar-

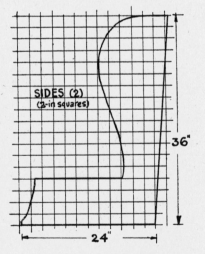

SIDES (2)
(2-in squares)

36″

24″

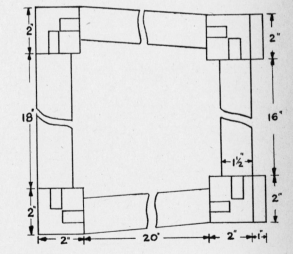

2″

18″

2″

2″

16″

1½″

2″

2″   20′   2″

rower boards, and an extra joint, will be called for. A feasible alternative to the t&g joints would be the insertion of three ⅜" x 1½" dowels in the 8" joint. Luckily we are able to stiffen the whole side with a pair of moulding strips running along the top edge as a support for the arm rest. At the bottom, the side portion will also be stiffened by a 3" trim board screwed to the frame and side. On the inside, too, the side is fastened to the seat frame, keeping it straight and rigid.

When the two wings and sides are completed, make the back and seat frames that hold them. Both these units have pinned open tenons at the ends of the side members and an ordinary tenon joint at the middle. The finished height of the back is 35¼" but another half-inch should be allowed to take care of the trimming, top and bottom, necessitated by the sloping back. The amount to be taken off one edge of the bottom can be gauged by

holding the back against the wing member, in line with the back slope. The excess will project below the bottom edge of the wing unit. The top excess can be removed after the back and sides are assembled. It is a good idea in making both back and seat frames to check them against the base for width, allowing 1½" for the two ¾" sides.

The back frame is attached to the wings by counterbore screws through the 2½" side members. With the wings supported by the back frame, the bottom frame can be inserted and screwed to the sides. The edges of both frames should be glued before screwing.

The upper portion is completed with the attachment of the arm rests. The two angle strips are glued, and screwed with 1½" No. 6 screws to the top edges of the sides. When the glue has set, the arms are attached with 1¼" No. 6 screws inserted at an angle through the angle strips from below and on alternate sides. The finished seat assembly can now be mounted as a unit on the base.

The frame is screwed directly to the base side and front members with 1¾" No. 12 screws. The junction of the base and upper part is concealed

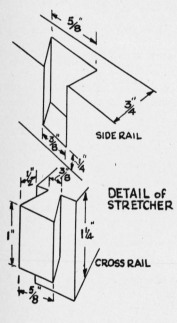

SIDE RAIL

DETAIL of STRETCHER

CROSS RAIL

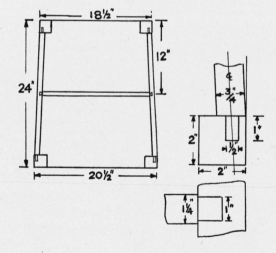

by the 3" wide finishing strips, mitered at the corners. The side strips need to be shaped slightly on the inside face at the ends to take care of the angle between the legs and the frame side-members. They are attached with countersink screws to the frame and to the sides, the back frame, and the front edge of the seat frame. At the front the trim board exends up ⅝" above the frame to cover the front edge of the upholstery frame. This sets the height for the rest of the trim.

The chair is upholstered by applying webbing, cotton, horsehair, muslin, and covering material to the two upholstery frames and setting them in position.

The back frame is held at the top by extending the cover material over the top of the chair back frame and bringing it down to the bottom of that frame and securing it there with the trim board. Several alternatives to this method will suggest themselves.

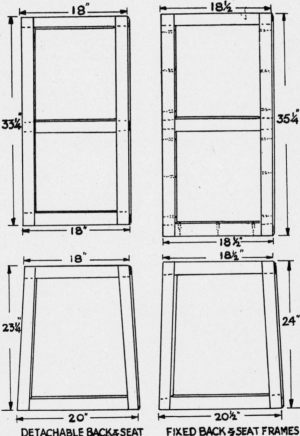

DETACHABLE BACK & SEAT   FIXED BACK & SEAT FRAMES

CHAISE LONGUE

Wood: Pine or oak.

Material Requirements:

> Legs—Two pieces 2" x 2" x 19". two pieces 2" x 2" x
> 18", two pieces 2" x 4" x 38".
> Side Rails—Two pieces ¾" x 5" x 63".
> End Rails—Two pieces ¾" x 5" x 18".
> Transverse Stretchers—Three pieces ½" x 1½" x 19½".
> Principal Stretchers—Four pieces ½" x 1½" x 36".
> Back—Two pieces 1½" x 1½" x 19½".
> Dowels—Four pieces ⅜" x 2½".

Procedure:

Make legs first, starting with the back ones which govern certain dimensions of the others. These can be cut out of planks 2" x 6" x 38" most economically, after marking out as shown in drawing. Sand back of center portion into a curve, and curve ends of front faces into the face of the side-rail mortise section. Do not sand off the top of the leg until after the top rail has been fitted.

Because the side rails call for deep mortises, the head rail is attached by dowels which do not weaken the back as much as a second mortise would. These dowels do not go entirely through the side of the leg, but they serve to lock the side-rail tenons in place. For this reason the head rail cannot be assembled until the side rails are made and

put together, and the dowel holes then drilled.

The back of the seat is formed with a pair of rabbeted cross-bars tenoned into the stiles. The rabbets are intended to receive an upholstered plywood back, or a caned frame. The top rail can be fitted temporarily and its top front edge sanded off, together with the tops of the back legs, so that they are nicely rounded toward the front.

The other four legs are now cut, checking the height of the tenons and shoulders against the back leg mortises. The side-rail mortises in the back legs should be exactly 14½" from the floor, and since the side-rail tenon has a ½" shoulder, the bottom of the side rail itself will be 14" from the floor. The tenon in the bottom legs will therefore be 14½"

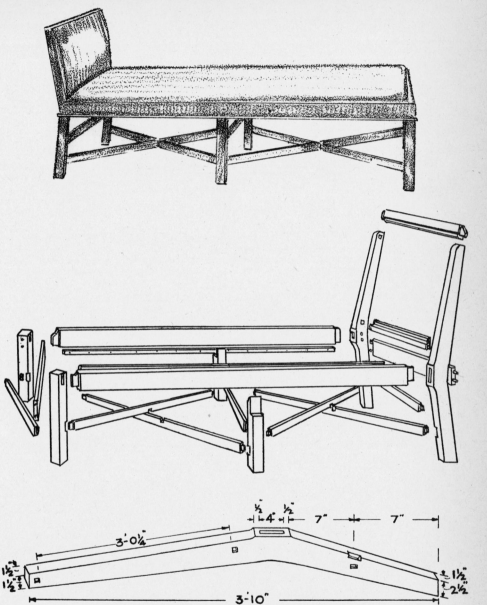

DETAIL OF BACK LEG & POST

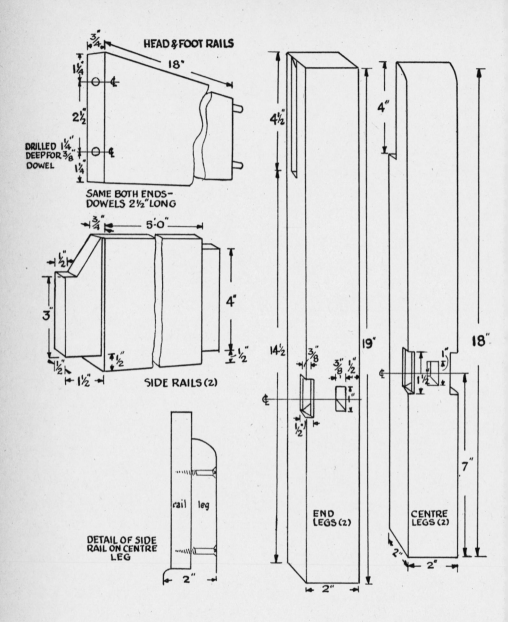

HEAD & FOOT RAILS

SAME BOTH ENDS—
DOWELS 2½" LONG

DRILLED 1¼"
DEEP FOR ⅜"
DOWEL

SIDE RAILS (2)

DETAIL OF SIDE
RAIL ON CENTRE
LEG

rail   leg

END
LEGS (2)

CENTRE
LEGS (2)

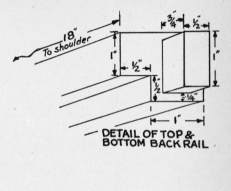

DETAIL OF TOP &
BOTTOM BACK RAIL

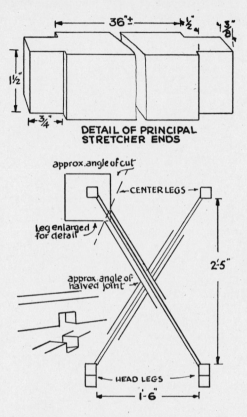

DETAIL OF PRINCIPAL
STRETCHER ENDS

approx. angle of cut

CENTER LEGS

Leg enlarged
for detail

approx. angle of
halved joint

2'-5"

HEAD LEGS

1'-6"

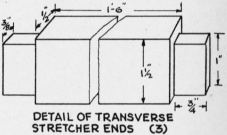

DETAIL OF TRANSVERSE
STRETCHER ENDS   (3)

from the floor, but the shoulders on the center legs will be only 14" from the bottom.

An important feature of the side rails is the haunched tenon at the foot end. This gives the extra width to resist sideways bending and at the same time is entirely concealed. In cutting the mortise for this in the leg, the holes are drilled as if the tenon was 3" high, spaced 1½" from the top of the leg. After these are cut to the proper depth and trimmed to the finished width, the angle cut is made down from the top into the hole which it enters ½" from the bottom. The tenon is cut to fit this mortise. Here again the foot rail is attached with dowels, the dowel holes being drilled while the tenon is in place.

After all six legs have been cut and fitted to the side rails, the set of three transverse stretchers is made. Each of these calls for a ⅜" x 1" mortise in each leg, all centered at 7" from the bottom. With these in position and the whole frame clamped together it is a simple matter to locate the main stretchers and measure their required lengths exactly. The angle at which each stretcher enters the leg can be seen, and marked, if the top and bottom lines are marked on the corners of the legs. If the whole frame assembly is turned upside down on a pair of horses this work will be simplified. The bottoms of the stretchers will be 6¼" from the bottoms of the legs—exactly in line with the cross-stretchers. Holding each stretcher in turn at this level (beween is own respective pair of legs) you can mark the distances each face will come either side the corner of the leg (presuming the stretcher tenons have not yet been cut). If this is found difficult, a short length of scrap wood, the size of the stretcher material, notched at the end to straddle the corner of the leg, may help in marking the side lines.

When all the legs have been marked, you can make fine saw cuts across the leg corners, inside the horizontal lines and extending to the vertical lines. These are the limits of the square face to be formed on the leg against which the stretcher shoulders will rest. This flat surface is now formed by chiseling out the waste between the saw cuts and along the vertical lines. In the centers of these rectangular spaces, the mortises are cut in the usual manner. After all mortises and tenons have been cut, the stretchers are marked for notching where they cross one another. This is easy to do if the frame assembly is stood on a large sheet of paper and the outlines of the legs marked on it. The frame is removed

and a stretcher placed in position and its outline marked. The other stretcher is then laid across this outline, joining the other pair of legs, and its outline also drawn. A bevel protractor is set to the angle at which the two pairs of lines cross and used in setting out the cut for the halved joint.

In the final assembly the side rails are first put together with their respective legs. Then the end rails, whose dowel holes have been drilled while the side tenons are in position, are attached to one side.

The stretchers likewise are placed in position on the same side. Finally, with all tenons and dowels glued, the other rail and leg assembly is attached to the loose ends of the cross members, and the whole clamped tightly in two directions. If all members are tight, the angle stretchers will prevent the frame being pulled out of square. What remains to be done depends upon the type of upholsered units to be employed. Usually the simplest and cheapest way is to screw and glue 1" x 1" strips to the inside of the side members to support a number of slats that will form a base for a loose cushion. Alternatively, a loose upholstered frame can be set in, in the same manner as the back.

MODERN BEDSTEAD

Wood: Pine and plywood.

Material Requirements:

Base—(Legs) Four pieces 2½" x 2½" x 12"; (rails) two pieces ⅞" x 5" x 75", two pieces ⅞" x 5" x 40"; (bearers) four pieces ¾" x 3" x 41¼"; 16 feet of ¾" x 1".

Head (Top rail) One piece ¾" x 3½" x 42"; (bottom rail) one piece ¾" x 3" x 37"; (stiles) two pieces ¾" x 2½" x 36½"; (posts) two pieces 1½" x 2½" x 46"; (back) one piece plywood ¼" x 34¼" x 37¾".

Procedure:

Start with base, first cutting four legs and marking out for mortises and cut-away corner. Cut corner first, removing wood 5" down from the top by 1" x 1". This leaves two faces, each 1½" wide, down the middle of which a ½" mortise is to be cut. But do not cut the mortises till the side and end rail tenons are finished. Next make the end rails of ⅞" stuff, 5" deep, 40" long. At each end form a 1½" x 4" tenon, ½" thick. From these tenons cut mortises to fit on the two pairs of legs. Then make side rails.

Side rails are a little more complicated, having four dovetail sockets cut into their bottom inside edge. The centers of the first and last bearer are 9" from the ends of the pieces. The centers of the other pair are 18" apart. Mark these centers but do not cut the dovetails yet. Finish the side rails by cutting the tenons, then mark off the mortises for them in the legs. Cut and fit them tightly to the mortises.

The bearers, cut from ¾" x 3" stock, are 41½" long. Note the sharp angle of the dovetails necessitated by the bending and consequent tension they are to undergo. Carefully match all four bearers for length between shoulders. Now turn the leg and rail assemblies over and fit them to the side rails. With the whole base upside down, use the bearer ends to mark out the dovetails on the centers previously indicated. While doing this, see that the base is exacly square by checking outside corners with a large steel square or measuring the leg centers

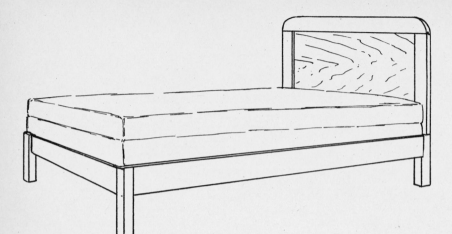

crosswise. Also check each bearer for squareness with the side rails. Disassemble and hold side rail in vise to cut dovetails. Cut as far as possible with a saw, then chisel out remainder. Fit all dovetails

and mark the boards for their final position. Glue and screw them to the side rails, then glue and assemble all tenons to the legs. Clamp the frame till glue is set.

Meanwhile the strips of ¾" x 1" can be glued and screwed between the bearers, between end bearers and legs, and laterally the whole width of the head and foot boards. These must all be level with the upper faces of the bearer so that each supports its own proportion of the total weight of the mattresses.

With the base made, the construction and addi-

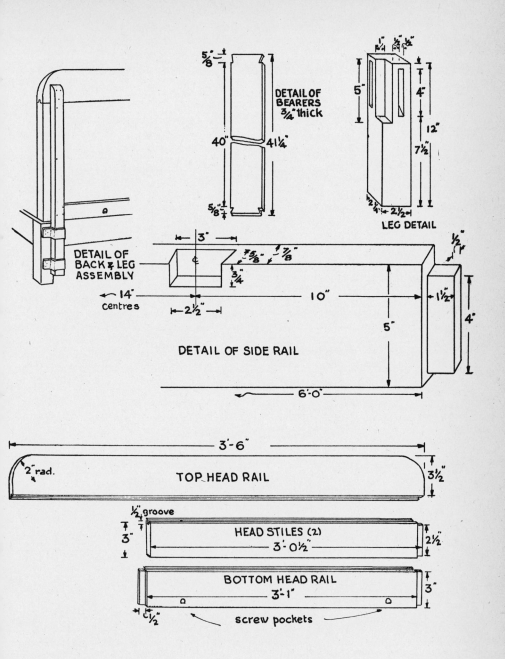

DETAIL OF
BEARERS
¾" thick

LEG DETAIL

DETAIL OF
BACK & LEG
ASSEMBLY

14"
centres

DETAIL OF SIDE RAIL

TOP HEAD RAIL

2" rad.

3½"

½" groove

HEAD STILES (2)
3'-0½"

BOTTOM HEAD RAIL
3'-1"

screw pockets

tion of the headboard is simple. It consists principally of a sheet of ⅜" plywood in a frame. The
frame has a 3½" wide top rail, a pair of 2½" wide
stiles, and a 3" bottom rail, all tongued together.
These pieces are all ¾" thick, and each inside edge
has a ⅜" groove ploughed in it, ½" deep, to receive
the plyboard. The top ends of the stiles have
tongues ½" long and ⅜" thick that fit into the top-
rail groove. The bottom rail has a similar tongue on
each end and these join the stile grooves. The
length of these tongues, properly glued, should give
sufficient anchorage, but they do not have to be
relied upon to hold the frame together. Two 1½" x
2½" posts are attached to the back of the headboard, projecting 10" below it. These are counterbored and screwed to the top rail, the stile and the
bottom rail, tying them rigidly together. The plywood is not glued in the grooves.

The whole head assembly rests on the top bed
rail and is supported by a pair of wrought-iron
brackets on the back of each leg. In addition, any
possible movement is checked by running two No. 9,
2" screws through the bottom head rail into the bed
rail. For this purpose, two screw pockets are formed
in the usual manner, an inch from the bottom edge
of the back rail.

This bedstead will accommodate a box spring
and an inner-spring or foam mattress. As in all
such cases, the mattresses should be bought first to
insure the frame being made large enough to fit.

LOW-POST BEDSTEAD

Wood: Pine or maple.

Material Requirements:

> Head Posts—Two pieces 3" x 3" x 42".
> Foot Posts—Two pieces 3" x 3" x 36".
> Side Rails—Two pieces 1" x 5" x 76".
> End Rails—Two pieces 1" x 5" x 40".
> Headboard—One piece ¾" x 19" x 39".
> Footboard—One piece ¾" x 14" x 39".
> Fillets—Two pieces 1" x 1" x 72", two pieces 1' x 1"
>   x 36".
> Slats—Six pieces 1" x 39".

Procedure:

Make the four posts first. Plane stock smooth all over and mark out for cutting. Rough out with saw and finish with chisel, using rasp for curve under top cap. After all work is finished they should be fine-sanded till all parts are perfectly smooth. At this time decide whether or not you want demountable joints for taking bed to pieces, and mark out posts accordingly. For permanent joints you can have pinned tenons or tenons secured with screwed angle plates. Demountable joints are best made with either bolts or sheet-metal hooks. Procedure in case of bolted joints is the same as in the tenon joint, i.e., a tenon is made first.

Mark out and cut a mortise on each post, 1½" deep for a tenon 3" wide and ¾" thick. In marking out, place all four posts side by side and mark top and bottom of mortise with a square across all faces, being sure that all post feet are exactly in line. With the screw type of joint these mortises need to be on the center line of the post and not to one side. This imposes limitations on the length of the tenons of the head and foot rails. These have to be no longer than 1⅛" and therefore should be pinned as well as glued. A ⅜" maple dowel will serve.

The bolt holes in head and foot posts should just clear the ½" bolts, and be counterbored ¾" to sink the heads. This will leave ¾" of wood between the bolt-head and tenon to take the strain. Head and foot boards are laid out on 1" squares and

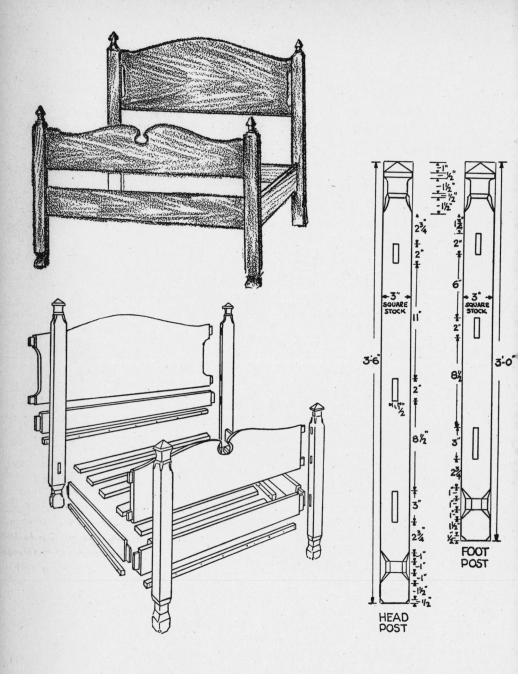

HEAD
POST

FOOT
POST

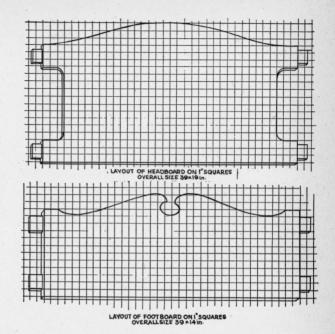

LAYOUT OF HEADBOARD ON 1" SQUARES
OVERALL SIZE 39×19 in.

LAYOUT OF FOOTBOARD ON 1" SQUARES
OVERALL SIZE 39×14 in.

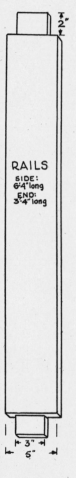

RAILS

SIDE:
6'-4" long
END:
3'-4" long

3"
5"
2"

cut with a scroll or band saw. The tenons here can be a full 1½" and if properly fitted and glued will not need planing. If it is necessary to joint two boards to provide the width required a glued t&g joint is recommended, with the tenons entering the posts being made a slightly loose fit vertically. This will obviate any shrinkage stress on the boards. It is particularly important to have the sides of these boards exactly parallel and at right angles to the base so that the shoulders of all four tenons will fit snugly against the posts. As an alternative, ½" plywood can be used for these boards, in which case the side fit of the tenons must be tight. The ply tenons are best tapered very slightly top and bottom so that they make a tight joint, but all four must fit the mortises equally well.

With all joints formed, the head and footboards and their respective rails can be glued and clamped

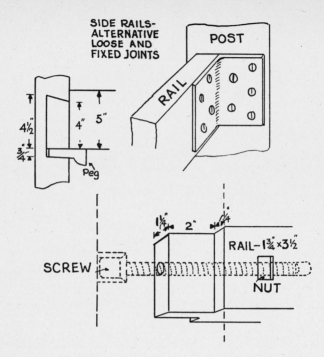

into their posts, and pinned. Before the side rails are assembled, the strips of 1" x 1" should be glued and screwed to them, in line with their bottom inside edges. At least six screws should be used to each side. If a box spring is used that fits snugly against the end rails, similar strips can be used on these rails to take some of the weight and obviate tipping. The principal load, however, is taken by the slats that rest on the side strips. If head and foot strips are used they should of course be 1" up from the bottom edge so as to be level with the tops of the slats. These strips also serve to stiffen the side and end rails against bending outward. The slats

can be of spruce and should be cut to exact length so that they will rest on the 1 x 1's without bulging the sides yet having a maximum bearing on the strips. For this reason special care needs to be taken to see that the ends of the slats are absolutely square.

NOTE: The simplest form of detachable rail has a half-dovetail tenon, with a wedge or key to force it up into the upper part of the mortise, as in the drawing. More modern is the thin metal hook sandwiched into a saw cut in the rail end and engaging one, or two, metal pins through a similar saw cut in the post.

TALL-POST BEDSTEAD

Wood: Pine, maple, walnut, or mahogany.

Material Requirements:

> Posts—Two pieces 4" x 4" x 76", two pieces 4" x 4" x 65",
>   two pieces 4" x 4" x 20", two pieces 4" x 4" x 30".
> Side Rails—Two pieces 1" x 5" x 76".
> End Rails—Two pieces 1" x 5" x 58".
> Headboard—One piece ¾" x 10" x 58".
> Steel Connectors—Four ⅛".
> Steel Pins—Eight.
> Dowels—Four 1¼' x 8".
> Iron Hangers—Eight.
> Iron Bolts—Four ¼" x 3¼".
> Canopy Rods—Four pieces 1" x 1½" x 60", two pieces 1" x
>   1½" x 78".
> Finials—Four 1½" x 3".

Procedure:

The posts of this bed are made in two parts for structural reasons, and this makes it possible to construct the head and foot assemblies as permanent units for strength and convenience. The posts are made first, and in this design no turning is called for. Each post is in two sections, as shown in the drawings, joined together by heavy dowels. The dowels are fixed in the upper part and detachable from the lower part. The bed can therefore be used either as a low-post or tall-post type. In the former case all that would be needed would be 2 pairs of caps for the posts.

The upper sections of the posts can be made from a 7" wide plank, 4" thick, or even a narrower one if the grain runs parallel with the centers of the posts. After they have been roughly ripped out, the posts are marked on all four sides and the ends to produce an octagonal column 4" thick at the base and ¾" thick at the top. The best procedure is to rip out the post from the 4" plank so that you have a 4" thick piece tapering to ¾". This gives a square tapered post which is easily made into an octagon by planing off the four corners till all sides are equal in width. One inch from the

bottom of each post the sides are beveled off as shown. The bottom sections of the posts are kept square, with the lower 10″ tapered to a 2″ foot.

Joining the two parts of each post requires extreme care. The dowel hole is large and must be exactly parallel to the center. It is simple to mark the center of the square section by drawing lines from corner to corner, but less easy on the octagonal piece unless all eight sides are equally wide. That center, of course, can be marked while the post is still square. Another important point is to see that both the butt end of the post and the top end of the lower section are exactly square with their centers. A slight variation here makes a big difference in six feet, and the post must not lean at all. The drilling of the dowel holes, in most cases, will have to be done horizontally, and a jig of some sort will need to be used to ensure that the holes do not wander or exceed their proper depth. The

dowel should be a fairly tight fit in the holes, and have a saw kerf along each side of the upper half to allow escape of air and excess glue. It will only be glued into the top section. Both ends of the dowel should be rounded off, and the edges of the holes slightly chamfered. The post tops are finished by drilling the top end for a metal screw to hold the curtain bar and finial. After fitting, the upper sections are laid aside until the rest of the bed is completed. Next, all mortises should be cut in the lower sections.

Several alternative methods of rail construction can be used. Generally the plain mortise and tenon is not satisfactory. Such beds need to be demountable and the old-time shallow heavy side rail with long bolts is an advantage. A good alternative is to use the 1″ x 5″ side rails and attach 4″ x 5″ blocks, 1½ thick, to their inner ends, with metal connector plates sandwiched between the two. These plates have jaws which engage with metal rods (or heavy screws) inside a narrow mortise in the post. These metal connectors can be either bought ready for use or cut from pieces of ⅛" steel plate and drilled for the attaching screws.

To assemble this device, the plate is held against the end of the side rail, projecting beyond it the depth of the slots. The positions of the screw are marked through the screw holes and the holes made through the rail and countersunk. The plate is now placed on the inside of the rail, the 1½" block laid on the other side of it, and the screws inserted and tightened. For best results the plate should be let into the thicker block and the surrounding wood glued. The slot in the post to receive the connector is made either with a small-diameter circular saw or drilled and chiseled out with a ⅛" mortise chisel. The height of the slot must be sufficient to clear the connector when it is raised to slip over the pins. The pins can be ordinary, heavy screws inserted from the inside face of the leg. The depth of the side rail calls for a connector almost as wide and having a pair of slots for two separate pins, one above the other, as indicated in the sketch. This will prevent any twisting of the rail. The head and end boards are tenoned and assembled as usual, as nearly flush with the other faces of the posts as possible to make room for the demountable joints on the other faces. Old-time beds of this type usually had solid rails up to 4" square, drilled for a rope "spring." If the

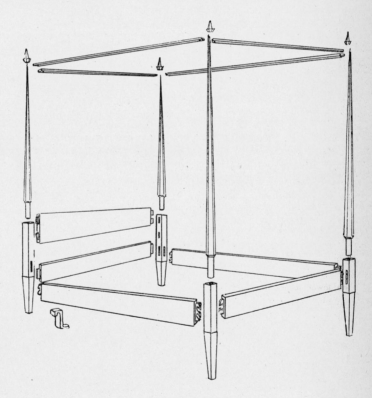

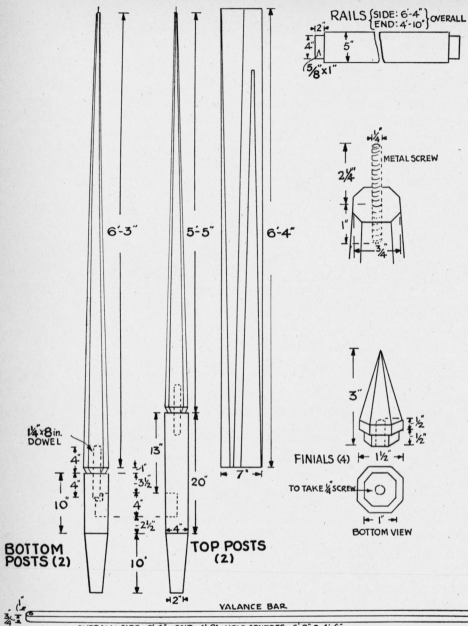

RAILS { SIDE: 6'-4" } OVERALL
       { END: 4'-10" }

5/8" x 1"

METAL SCREW

2¼"

1"

¾"

3"

½"
½"

FINIALS (4)   1½"

TO TAKE ¼" SCREW

1"

BOTTOM VIEW

6'-3"   5'-5"   6'-4"

1¼" x 8 in.
DOWEL

4"

4"

10"

7"

13"

1"
3½"

4"

2½"   4"

20"

BOTTOM
POSTS (2)

TOP POSTS
(2)

10"

2"

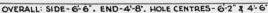

VALANCE BAR

¾"

OVERALL: SIDE - 6'-6". END - 4'-8". HOLE CENTRES - 6'-2" & 4'-6"

bolt-type fastening is preferred, these rails can be substituted, preferably not more than 1¾' x 3½" in section. If necessary the box spring can then be mounted directly on the rails.

The valance or curtain bars are drilled for the screws in the post tops. These screws can be cut out of ¼" bolts, and screwed into the holes made only slightly under ¼" diameter. The finials can be threaded in a similar manner. Any blacksmith will make the mattress suspension hooks which can hook over the top of the 1" side rail or be screwed to it. The post feet are best finished with domes of silence.

WELSH DRESSER

Wood: Pine.

Material Requirements:

Base—(Frame) One piece ¾" x 2" x 50", four pieces ¾" x 2" x 33", two pieces ¾" x 1½" x 60"; (end boards) two pieces ¾" x 14¼" x 29"; (partitions) two pieces ¾" x 14⅜" x 29".

Top—One piece 1" x 15¾" x 61½".

Back—Twenty-seven sq. ft. of ⅝" t&g.

Battens—Two pieces ¾" x ¾" x 11½", two pieces ¾" x 1½" x 11½".

Shelves—Two pieces ¾" x 13⅝" x 16¼".

Drawer Framing—(Front rails) Three pieces ¾" x 1½" x 25", one piece ¾" x ¾" x 25; (fillers) two pieces ½" x ½" x 4½", two pieces ½" x ½" x 7⅜", four pieces ½" x ½" x 6".

Slides and Guides—Six pieces ¾" x 1" x 13⅜", eight pieces ½" x ½" x 12⅞", one piece ¾" x 1¼" x 25", one piece ⅝" x 13⅝" x 25".

Doors—(Panels) Two pieces ⅞" x 10¾" x 26⅞"; (stiles) four pieces ¾" x 2" x 30⅛"; (rails) four pieces ¾" x 2" x 30⅛"; (rails) four pieces ¾" x 2" x 14".

Knobs—Ten turned wood 1¼".

H-Hinges—Four 3".

Turnbuttons—Two wood.

Drawers—

Front—One piece ¾" x 4½" x 24", two pieces ¾" x 6" x 24", one piece ¾" x 7⅜" x 24".

Backs—One piece ½" x 4⅛" 24", two pieces ½" x 5⅝" x 24", one piece ½" x 7" x 24'.

Sides—Two pieces ½" x 4½" x 13⅝", two pieces ½" x 6" x 13⅝", one piece ½" x 7⅜" x 13⅝".

Bottoms—Four pieces plywood ⅛" x 13" x 23¼".

Top—(Ends) Two pieces ¾" x 8" x 40"; (shelves) three pieces ¾" x 4½' x 58⅞".

Back—Twenty-five ft. of ½" x 8" t&g (17 sq. ft.).

Frieze—One piece ⅝" x 5" x 60".

Crown Moulding—Nine ft. of 4½".

Glue Blocks—Eight 2".

Plywood—One piece ¼" x 17½" x 65".

Dowels—Six ⅜" x 2".

Procedure:

For base proceed as follows: Make up boards of required width for the two ends and two partitions. You will probably use two boards for each, glued butt joints will serve. Tops of the end boards are reinforced with ¾" x 1½" battens, glued and screwed, 1½" side up. These take the screws to hold the base top. The partition boards have ¾" x ¾" battens which are not attached to the base top

at all, but stiffen the partition against warping. At the ends of these stiffeners, the two partitions are notched to receive the longitudinals. At the same time, the ends of the front top rail are dovetailed into the end boards. The dimensions of this joint should be carefully noted. The mortises for the tenons are formed on each end of the stiles which are jointed into the base member of the frame and the top member, and the whole is assembled to the end boards and fastened by screws down through the top rails.

Set in ⅝" to clear the back boards is the back top rail. This is glued and secret-screwed to the end boards as shown. The inside face of the end boards is dadoed for the shelves, the center line being 17" from the bottom of the board. The facing side of the partitions also is dadoed at that level, not more than ⅛" deep. This dado is stopped ⅝" from the back edge so that it will not show when the back is installed.

The shoulder partitions are now inserted, set in ½" from the drawer edges of the center stiles. They are fastened in the same manner as the end boards. In all cases the stiles are glued to the front edges of the transverse boards, and held to them by finishing nails driven through the faces of the stiles. The small nail holes are later filled with wood paste.

On either side of the center drawer section, cleats are screwed to the bottom front rail, end board, and partition, to support the ⅝" cupboard bottom

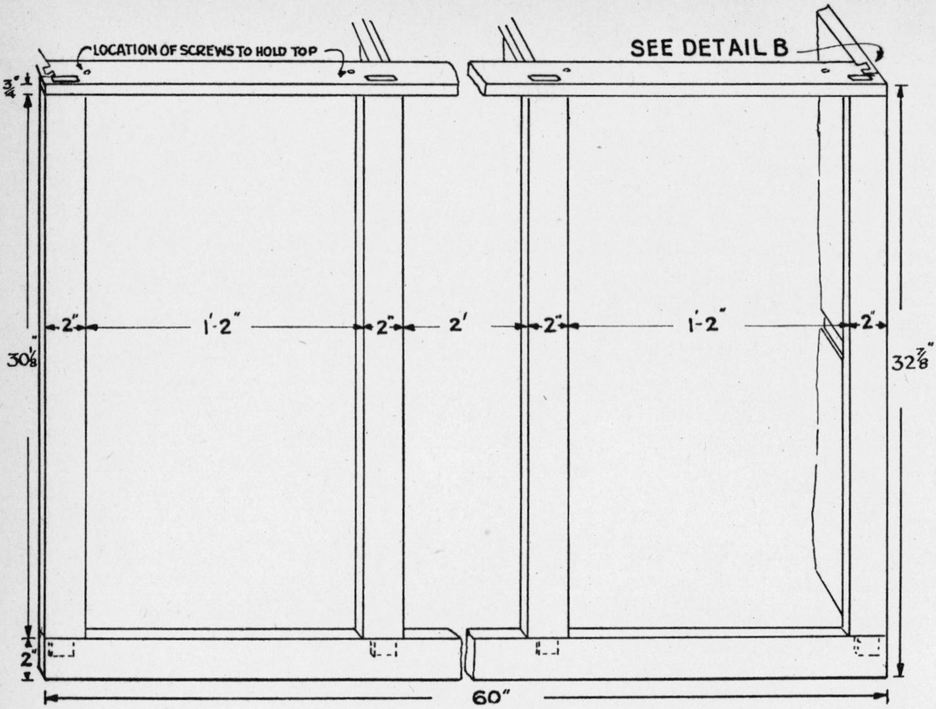
LOCATION OF SCREWS TO HOLD TOP
SEE DETAIL B
3/4"
30 1/8"
2"
1'-2"
2"
2'
2"
1'-2"
2"
32 7/8"
2"
60"

FRONT FRAME

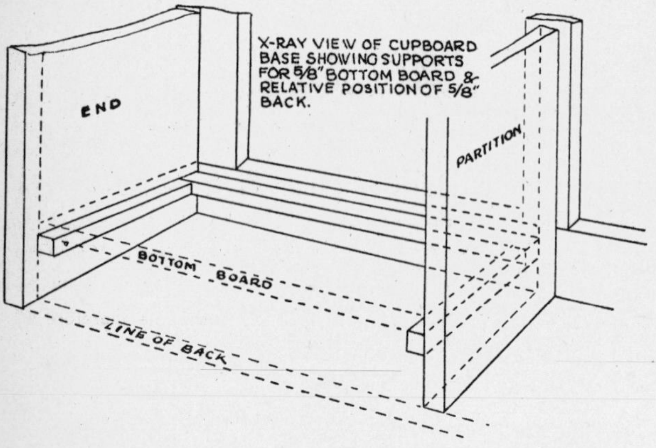
X-RAY VIEW OF CUPBOARD BASE SHOWING SUPPORTS FOR 5/8" BOTTOM BOARD & RELATIVE POSITION OF 5/8" BACK.
END
PARTITION
BOTTOM BOARD
LINE OF BACK

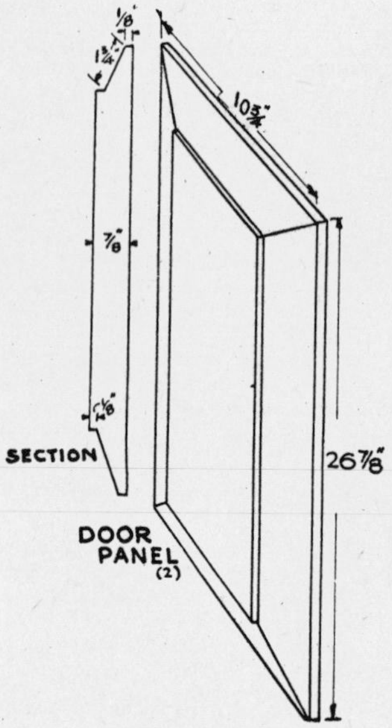
1/8"
1 3/4"
10 3/4"
7/8"
SECTION
26 7/8"
DOOR PANEL (2)

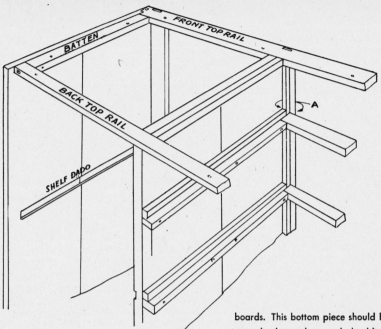

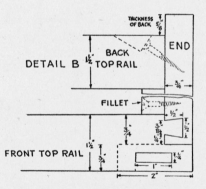

boards. This bottom piece should be one board, or two glued together, and should fit snugly on all three sides. The tops of the cleats are then glued and the board toenailed into the cleats and sides. It thus becomes a part of the structure, adding stiffness and forming an anchor for the back board when it is finally installed. The cupboard shelf is of course inserted in the dadoes before the partition is firmly attached.

The drawer supports are now inserted. Note that the drawers and their dividing rails are set back the thickness of the front stiles, i.e., ¾". The front rails, in fact, extend behind the stiles, from one partition to the other. The rails are therefore 1" longer than the drawer opening. These front pieces, however, are not inserted by themselves. After fitting for length they are assembled with their side members that are angle-tongued into them. These three pieces are inserted as a unit, with a little glue on the face of the front rail where it is to touch

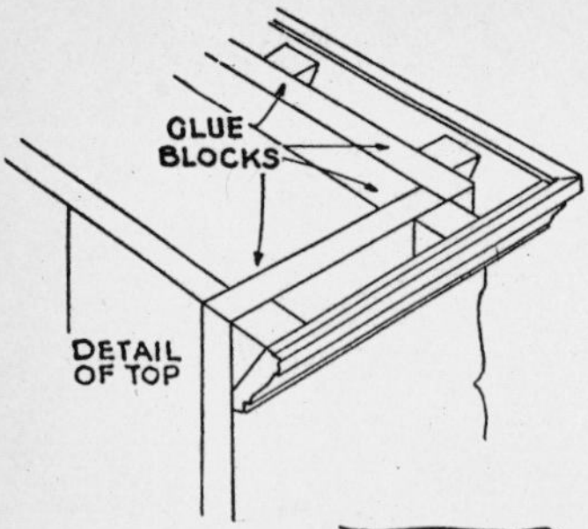
GLUE BLOCKS
DETAIL OF TOP

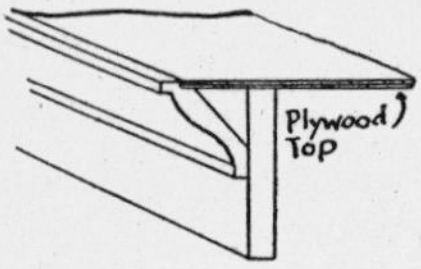
Plywood Top

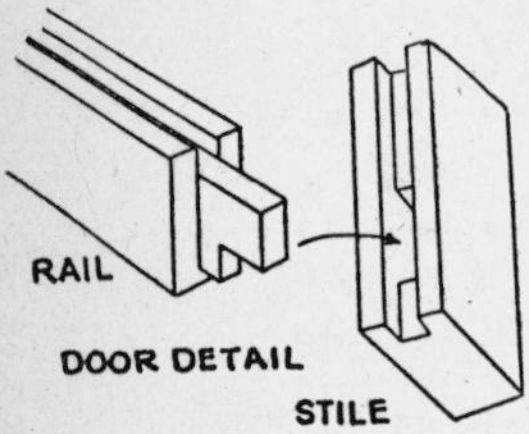
RAIL
DOOR DETAIL
STILE

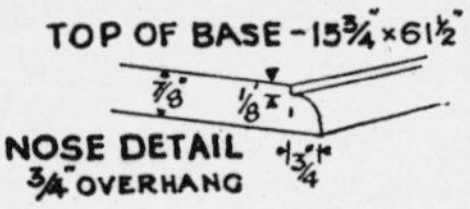
TOP OF BASE-15¾"×61½"
⅞
⅛"
NOSE DETAIL
¾" OVERHANG
¾

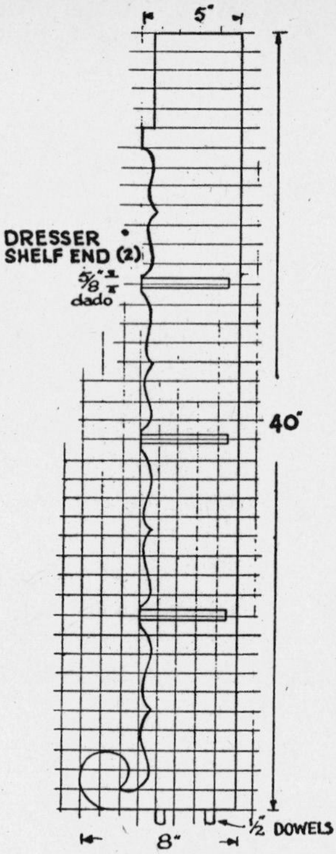
5"
DRESSER SHELF END (2)
⅝" dado
40"
8"
½" DOWELS

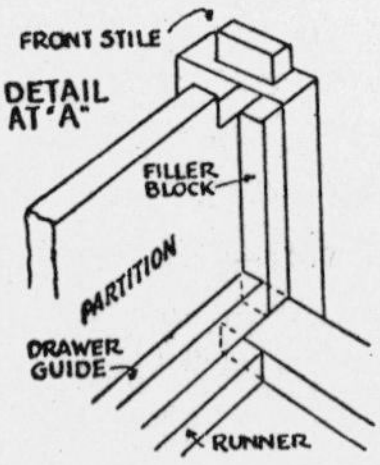
FRONT STILE
DETAIL AT "A"
FILLER BLOCK
PARTITION
DRAWER GUIDE
RUNNER

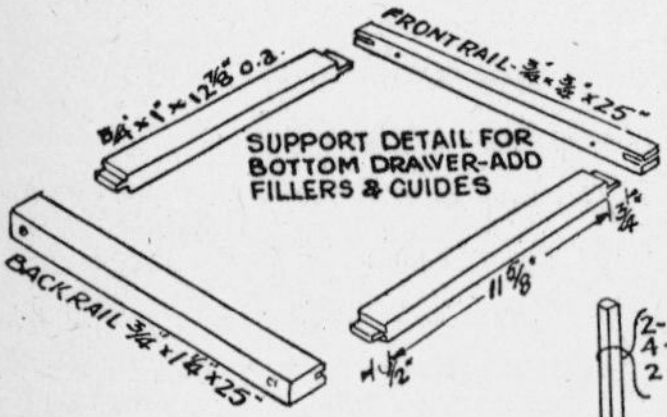
FRONT RAIL-¾"×¾"×25"
SUPPORT DETAIL FOR BOTTOM DRAWER-ADD FILLERS & GUIDES
BACK RAIL ¾"×1¼"×25"
11⅝"
½"

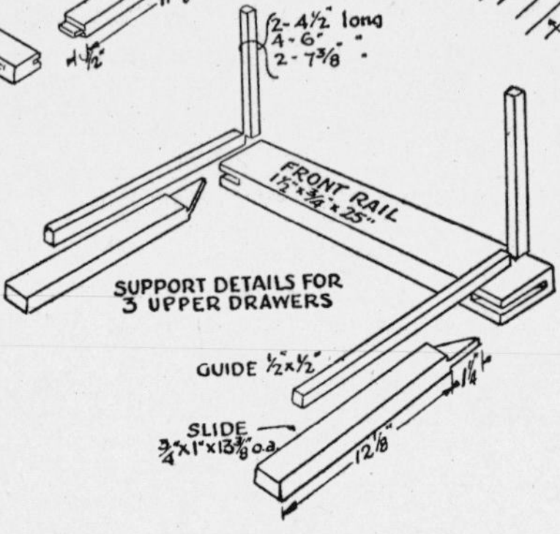
2-4½" long
4-6" " "
2-7⅜" "
FRONT RAIL 1½"×¾"×25"
SUPPORT DETAILS FOR 3 UPPER DRAWERS
GUIDE ½"×½"
SLIDE ¾"×1"×13⅜" o.a.
12⅛"
1¼"

the stiles. The rail is clamped to the stiles while the side pieces, already glued, are screwed to the partitions. Locating the rails is simplified if the little ½" x ½" filler blocks are cut first. These are glued in the corners behind the stiles and the front rails fitted to them. If the blocks are cut exactly to length the rail will automatically be at right angles to the stiles and the drawer openings therefore square. Similar blocks are laid in the angles of the runners to form guides for the drawers. In the case of the bottom drawer, the front rail goes behind the base strip (bottom rail) and through-tenons can be used for the runners. Guides are used here also, together with a back rail. This rail is pocketed at each end for screws that hold it to the two partitions. It serves to maintain the relative positions of the partitions. The final stage of carcase construction is the installation of the top, fastened by screws from below through the top rails and end battens. It is not glued on so that it can expand slightly. The doors are made and installed last, with panel grooves and shouldered tenons. The panels need to be fitted carefully so that they show the same margin all around. The inner edges of the doors can be relieved a little so that they will open and close without binding, but this should not be done till after the hinges have been installed. A shaving under the door while fitting the hinges will insure bottom clearance.

Some means of keeping the doors flush with the stiles when closed will be needed. The bottom board can be set up slightly for this, but it is a simple matter to install small wood stops, top and bottom, for the closed door to strike against. Normally the doors would be kept closed with wooden turnbuttons, but ball catches can be used to serve both purposes with small sacrifice of authenticity. There are no problems connected with the drawers, but care is necessary in making the front to fit the opening snugly.

The shelf unit can be varied in height to suit individual requirements without altering the general pattern. The side members call for careful work with the scroll (or band) saw, and the decorative foot should not be weakened by over-cutting the thinnest part. Since all shelves differ in height the length of the edge curves varies, but a good sweep can be achieved by the use of squared paper.

Note that the shelf dadoes are ⅛" thinner than the shelves. The shelf ends have ⅛" x ⅛" cut away from the top side to fit the dadoes. In fitting the shelves they must be of exactly the same length, and all three installed at the same time. Each is secured with glue and two 1½" No. 6 screws at each end, slightly counterbored. Before fitting the shelves, plough a triangular groove the full length of each shelf, about 1¼" from the back to hold plates, etc. As an alternative, ¼" square strips can be glued and bradded on, and the top arrises rounded off.

The fascia board is fitted next and then the crown moulding. The moulding must be fitted accurately in the miters but no tongue is necessary. Fine finishing nails will help the glued joints. Note that the top edge of the moulding is rabbeted ⅛" x ⅛" to take the plywood top. The moulding therefore is set up ⅛" above the top of the side and back and fascia boards and nailed to all three.

The back, comprised of ⅝" t&g boards, is fastened to the backs of the shelves and caught at the ends by finishing nails through the sides. The tongues should be glued, and a ¾" x 1" strip can be glued and screwed to the top of the boards, inside, as a batten and nailing strip for the plywood. A similar ½" x 1" batten at the bottom edge may make neater job.

The triangular glue-blocks that hold the crown moulding are inserted as soon as the moulding has been fixed in position, and should be level with the tops of sides and fascia boards. The blocks do not need nailing but the lower edges of the moulding can be reinforced with a few ¾" finishing nails.

Others can be applied through the plywood into the top of the moulding.

The top is held to the base by six ½″ dowels, 1½″ long. These are glued into the top unit but not into the bottom, so that the top can readily be removed. The top can be held more permanently by making two or more pockets in the back boards and screwing into the base top.

CHEST OF DRAWERS

Wood: Pine or maple and pine.

Material Requirements:

Carcase—
Ends—Two pieces ¾" x 15" x 44".
Top—One piece ¾" x 15¾" x 37½".
Bottom—One piece ¾" x 15" x 36".
Back—One piece ply ⅜" x 35" x 43½".
Front Rails—Five pieces ¾" x 3" x 35".
Back Rail—One piece ¾" x 3" x 43½".
Slides—Eight pieces ¾" x 1½" x 13⅛".
Center Hangers, Runners, etc.—Three ft. of ¾" x 3".
Guide—One piece ¾" x ¾" x 11⅝".
Feet—Two pieces 3" x 3¼" x 16½".
Base—Nine and a half ft. of ¾" x 3", one piece ¾' x 3" x 6".

Drawers—
Fronts—Two pieces 1¼" x 6" x 18", two pieces 1¼" x 8" x 36", two pieces 1¼" x 10" x 36.
Back—Two pieces ½" x 4¾" x 16⅞", two pieces ½" x 6¾" x 34⅞", two pieces ½" x 8¾" x 34⅞".
Sides—Four pieces ½" x 5¼" x 13¼", four pieces ½" x 7¼" x 14", four pieces ½" x 9¼" x 14".
Muntins—Four pieces ½" x 2¼" x 14".
Knobs—Ten 1½" x 2½" square, with screws and washers.

Procedure:

On this type of solid-ended carcase, the most important job is to make the dovetails, stopped dadoes, and mortises exact as to size and squareness. The end boards themselves therefore must be true and square, and in construction you have to allow for shrinkage which is not so important with paneled ends. The drawer runners, for example, must not be fastened securely to the end boards.

At the front end they are located by stub tenons into the front rails, and may be glued there, but the back end is held in the groove by a slotted screw hole that allows for expansion and contraction of the end board. The grooves keep the runners in line.

The ⅜" plywood back will not cover the ends of the runner grooves if it is fitted between the full thickness of the end boards. To make a really professional job, the end boards should be rabbeted to the depth of the runner dadoes so that the back board will cover them.

On all these chests, the very best construction

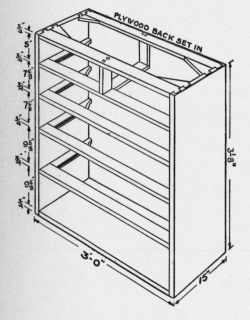

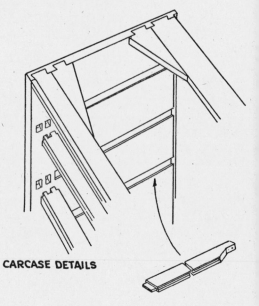

CARCASE DETAILS

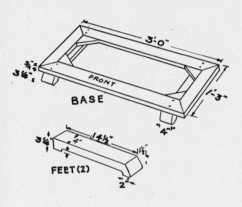

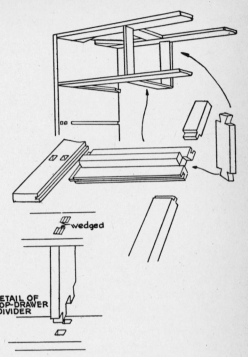

provides for dust boards between drawers. If you decide to use dust boards, which can be of very thin ply, it will be necessary to groove the front rails and the runners to receive them. If you do not use dust boards, the front rail need only be grooved at the points where the runners are stubtenoned into them.

The two top drawers call for a center runner and kicker. The double runner could be supported by a vertical bar or muntin fastened into the back top rail and the bottom board. All you need, then, is a groove in this board to hold the back end of the runner. This, however, shortens the other drawers by the thickness of the vertical board, though it helps stiffen the carcase. In place of the continuous board, a hanger, as shown, can be used

satisfactorily, and only the top pair of drawers will be shortened (from front to back). In this case, the runner is tongued into the front rail, glued, and held by a couple of nails driven in at an angle so that they will not easily pull out or loosen through the drawers striking the hanger.

It will be noticed that the drawers are lipped ⅜" all around so that the fronts just clear one another by ⅛" or so. This leaves very little of the front rails visible when the drawer is closed. If the chest is of maple these rails can be of pine, stained to match, but a better job is to face them with a ¼" strip of maple. The ends, of course, would be of solid maple.

The bottom of the chest is attached to the sides by lapped dovetails. The construction is similar to

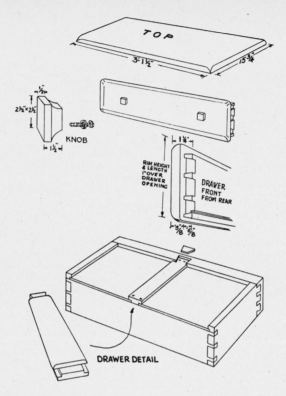

DRAWER DETAIL

that of the top, i.e., two pairs of dovetails, but the end boards are rabbeted between these dovetails, and the bottom board held in the rabbet with glue and screws. As an alternative the bottom can be dovetailed right across, preferably with small dovetail pins at each end and wider ones in the middle. The small dovetails help to keep the end boards from curling outward.

The construction of the base offers no problems, but the corner miters should be fastened with dowels as well as corner blocks, and the whole screwed firmly to the bottom board of the carcase, using slotted holes at the back and no glue.

The top of the chest is attached by screwing up through front and back rails, and this may be glued and clamped, because any expansion will be nearly the same as that of the end boards to which the rails are attached.

The drawer muntins are simple to make. Cut the grooves first, to accommodate thickness of drawer bottoms, then form lap and dovetail, finally rounding off the corners of the face that goes inside the drawer. After the top and the drawer fronts have been finished and assembled, they can be rounded off at edges and corners to give the rustic effect as shown.

FRAMED DESK

Wood: Pine, maple, or walnut.

Material Requirements:

Frame—Nine ft. of 1" x 3", eighteen ft. of ¾" x 3", twenty-five ft. of ¾" x 2½".

Top—One piece ¾" x 21¾" x 45½".

Leaves—Two pieces ¾" x 21¾" x 22".

Base—One piece ¾" x 3¼" x 66", one piece ¾" x 2" x 63", one piece 3" x 3" x 10".

Moulding—Nine and one-half ft. of ¾" ogee.

Plywood—Two pieces ¼" x 18¾" x 26", two pieces ¼" x 21" x 21", two pieces ¼" x 10½" x 26."

Brackets—Two pieces ¾" x 12" x 30".

Bracket Hinges—Eight ¾" x 2".

Leaf Hinges—Six 1½" x 2".

Drawers—

Slides—Fourteen pieces ¾" x 1½" x 20", fourteen pieces ¾" x 3" x 17", fourteen pieces ¾" x ¾" x 13½".

Fronts—One piece 1" x 3½ x 18⅛", two pieces 1" x 3½" x 9", two pieces 1" x 5" x 9", two pieces 1" x 6" x 9", two pieces 1" x 7¾" x 9".

Sides—(See text)

Backs—Two pieces ½" x 3" x 9", one piece ½" x 3" x 18⅛", two pieces ½" x 5½" x 9", two pieces ½" x 7¼" x 9".

Bottoms—One piece ⅛" x 17⅝" x 20½", eight pieces ⅛" x 8½" x 20½".

Knobs (round)—Nine 1½".

Felt for Brackets—Two pieces ¾" x 1".

Procedure:

This carcase is entirely framed, the ends and inside faces of kneehole being filled in with ½" plywood. The first step is to make four transverse frames. In each case the front stiles are ¼" thicker than the horizontal and rear members to allow for the ply panel. The end front stiles are rabbeted back ½" to take the plywood, but in the case of the kneehole frames the ply finishes flush against the back face of the stiles. In all four cases the ply ends extend ¼" beyond the backs of the two pedestals to form a rabbet into which the two

back panels fit. These back panels are then flush with the backs of the bases and covered by the top. The rail that goes under the top drawers is halved or notched into the two kneehole stiles so that it forms an unbroken line right across the desk. The three middle 3" front rails have widely spaced double tenons to ensure they do not rock—a much better and stronger system than a single wide tenon.

The four sets of drawer slides in each pedestal are screwed to the rear stile at their back end; at the forward end they tongue into the rails. At

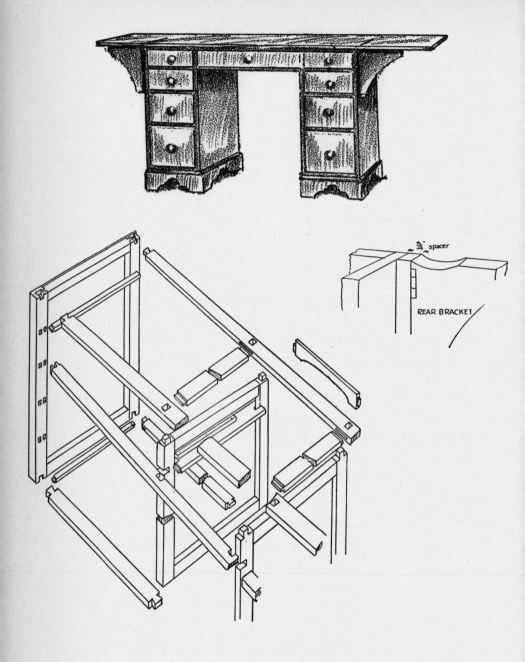

3/4" spacer

REAR BRACKET

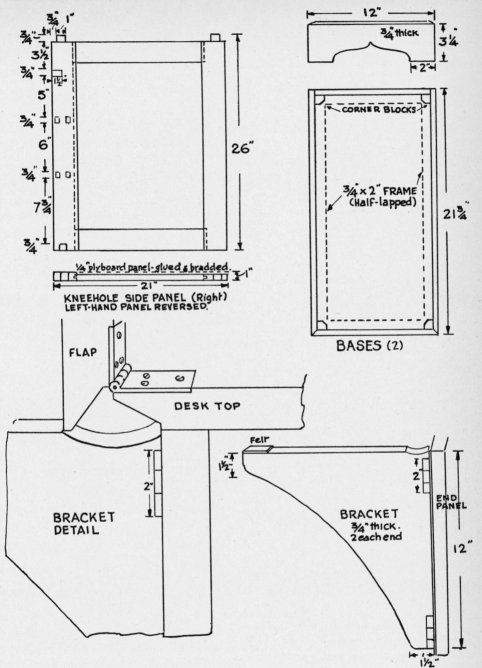

3/4" 1"
3/4"
3/4"
3 1/2"
3/4"
7"
1 1/2"
5"
3/4"
6"
3/4"
7 3/4"
3/4"
26"

1/4" plyboard panel-glued & bradded.
1"
21"
KNEEHOLE SIDE PANEL (Right)
LEFT-HAND PANEL REVERSED.

12"
3/4" thick
3 1/4
2"

CORNER BLOCKS
3/4" × 2" FRAME
(Half-lapped)
21 3/4"

BASES (2)

FLAP
DESK TOP
2"
**BRACKET
DETAIL**

Felt
1 1/2"
2"
**BRACKET
3/4" thick.
2 each end**
END PANEL
12"
1 1/2"

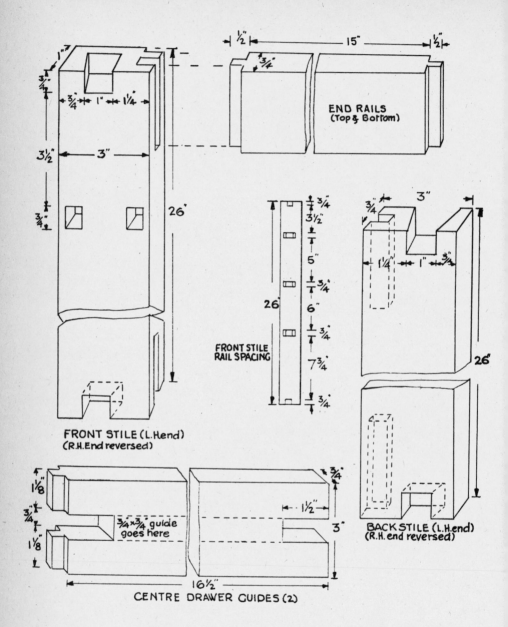

END RAILS
(Top & Bottom)

FRONT STILE
RAIL SPACING

FRONT STILE (L.H.end)
(R.H.End reversed)

BACK STILE (L.H.end)
(R.H. end reversed)

¾ x ¾" guide
goes here

CENTRE DRAWER GUIDES (2)

the bottom, however, the runner is screwed to the lower side rail and tongued at both ends. The pair of wide 3" transverse pieces at each side of the kneehole serve as kickers for all three top drawers. Both top and bottom, front and rear, rails are dovetailed into the stiles.

To stiffen the kneehole section of the structure, a deep (7") shaped member is inserted in the frame to form the back of the center drawer opening. This is tenoned at each end, and fastened strongly to the rear longitudinal with glue and screws. The continuous rail below the front of the top drawers, notched into the stiles, serves the same purpose there, so there should be no relative movement between the two pedestal units, nor any tendency for the center drawer to bind on an uneven floor.

A special feaure of this desk is the double top which opens out to about 86½". Three strong hinges should be used to each leaf, with two heavy brackets at each end. Where possible, the screws should go through into the stiles. Note that the length of the hinged joint is equal to the thickness of the top leaves, ¾".

The rear brackets should be mounted on strips ¾" x 1½". This will enable them to fold flat over the front brackets. The rear brackets must then be made ¾" narrower than the front ones.

All other edges of the top and leaves are kept square so that they come together and appear neat when the leaves are folded.

The two bases offer no complications. They provide for a ¾" ogee moulding in the angle between the three sides of each base and the upper edge of the pedestal feet.

A simple refinement can be added to this design by making the drawers ¼" longer and chamfering their fronts to that depth.

CORNER CUPBOARD

Wood: Pine.

Material Requirements:

Frame—Seventeen ft. of 1" x 5½", eighteen ft. of 1" x 3½", fifty-two ft. of ¾" x 3", twenty-two ft. of ¾" x 2½".

Shelves—(Plywood) One piece ½" x 44" x 44" (triangular), one piece ⅜" x 48" x 48" (triangular), one piece ⅝" x 48" x 48" (triangular), three pieces ½" x 48" x 48' (triangular).

Panels—(Plywood) Two pieces ¼" x 10" x 20½".

Crown Moulding—Five ft. of 4½".

Moulding—Five ft. of 1' x 2" nosing.

Retaining Strip—Seven and one-half feet of ½" x 1½".

Corner Blocks—Seven 1" thick.

Top Cleat—Three ft, of ¾" x ¾".

Glazed Door Frame—Eleven feet six inches of ¾" x 2".

Lower Door Frame (2)—Eighteen ft. of ¾" x 2".

Glazing Bar—Eleven ft. of ¾" x ¾". Square stock or ¾" ready-made bar.

Corner Shelf Supports—Nine ft. of 4" x 4".

Glass—Nine panes 7½" x 11" approx..

Brass Hinges—Six 1½" x ¾".

Latch, Lock, Knob, etc.

Procedure:

The only critical operation is the dovetailing of the top front rail into the base stiles. The base consists of two frames, joined together at 90 degrees to form the back corner, held across the front by the bar which dovetails into the front uprights of these frames and into the corner stiles. This fitting is best done after the frames are made and assembled to the stiles by pocketed screws and corner blocks. With the frames and stiles thus rigidly held together it is possible to insert the front frame in position between them and clamp the whole solidly together. Note that the main stiles have their inner face beveled to 45 degrees. The top rail can be laid in position and its ends marked off flush with the sides. The ends are then cut to shape and the dovetail pins scribed back to the thickness of the stiles and frame. With the dovetail pins cut, the rail is again laid in position and used as a jig for outlining the dovetails. Three pockets are made in the rail for screws to hold it to the front frame. The whole is locked firmly together by the plywood base which is screwed to the corner blocks and a strip fastened to the back of the front frame. A strip of 1½" moulding is used to cover the edges of the plywood top in front, and a plain strip along the two back panels. This moulding is set up about ⅜" to cover the joint between the upper and lower sections of the cupboard. The doors are fitted last, and the meeting stiles are rabbeted ½" and fitted either with key lock or ball catches top and bottom. If a lock is used, no knob need be fitted.

The top section of the cupboard is constructed in a somewhat different manner because it has no great weight to support. No dovetailing is used, the top and bottom boards providing the necessary attachment and support. Note, too, that the door frame stiles are attached to the main stiles with slip tongues, and the sides are rabbeted into the main stiles. It is usual to let these stiles, both top and bottom, project slightly beyond the backs so that they fit closer to the walls which are often slightly irregular.

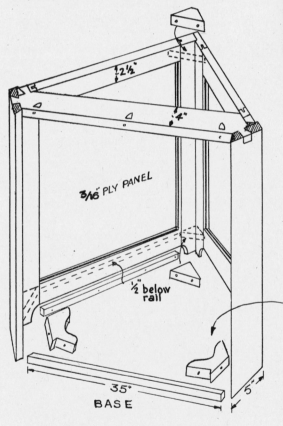

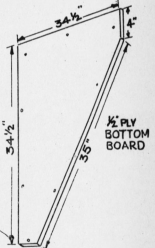

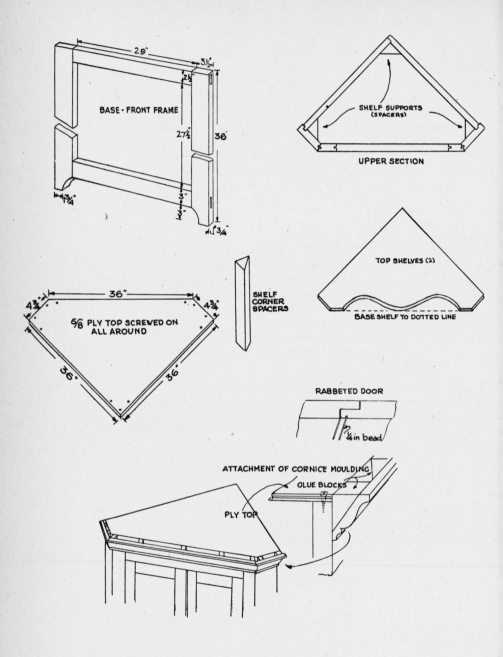

BASE - FRONT FRAME

29"
3½"
2½"
27½"
36"
3"
1¾"
1¾"

SHELF SUPPORTS
(SPACERS)

UPPER SECTION

36"
4¾"
4¾"
⅝ PLY TOP SCREWED ON
ALL AROUND
36"
36"

SHELF
CORNER
SPACERS

TOP SHELVES (2)

BASE SHELF TO DOTTED LINE

RABBETED DOOR

¼ in bead

ATTACHMENT OF CORNICE MOULDING

GLUE BLOCKS

PLY TOP

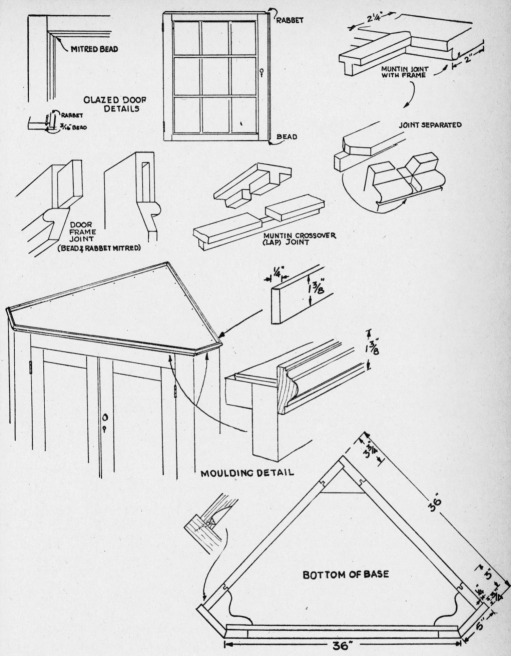

MITRED BEAD

GLAZED DOOR
DETAILS

RABBET
3/16" BEAD

RABBET

BEAD

2 1/4"

2"

MUNTIN JOINT
WITH FRAME

JOINT SEPARATED

DOOR
FRAME
JOINT
(BEAD & RABBET MITRED)

MUNTIN CROSSOVER
(LAP) JOINT

1/4"

1 3/8"

1 3/8"

MOULDING DETAIL

BOTTOM OF BASE

3 3/4

36"

5"

5 3/4

5"

36"

The interior of the upper section will look better if the sharp inside angles are eliminated. Therefore it is a good idea to support the shelf or shelves on triangular blocks or fillets fitted into the corners. These blocks are inserted both below and above the shelves, and can be cut conveniently from lengths of 4" x 4" material. The upper shelf should be shaped at the front and screwed firmly in position. The crown moulding is mitered at 67½ degrees and held with glue and nails at the bottom and glue-blocks at the top.

The glazed doors are made up with frames beaded on the inner edge and tenoned through— the bead being mitered and the back rabbeted ¼"

for the glass. The temporarily assembled frame is then marked out for glazing bars. These bars are plain and very simple to make from ¾" square stock rabbeted into T-shape. Their ends are mitered into the rabbet of the frame and extend into the body about ½".

The glass can be held either with glazier's points and putty or by ¼" triangular strips of wood bradded in place. Mitered at the corners, these strips make a neater job than the putty. The door closing edge needs no rabbet, but a ¼" strip should be glued and pinned to the closing stile, and a key lock is recommended here, or a knob and interior turnbutton.

B. BUILT-IN FURNITURE

The distinction between fixed and movable pieces may not be as simple as it appears. Ordinarily, a piece of built-in furniture, such as a cupboard or a set of shelves, is fitted into a certain space and is permanently attached to walls or partitions so that each becomes a part of the other. Walls and ceilings may form an essential part of the unit, and there is no objection to this provided the structure is definiely intended to be permanent. However, in many houses today, there is a likelihood of them changing hands sooner or later, and if the unit has to be remodeled or dismantled the walls may be seriously damaged in the process.

Therefore, in most cases it pays to consider just how far this process of building-in should be carried. One alternative is to construct the unit so that it needs no permanent and firm attachment to the surrounding fabric. Another is to build the piece as a complete unit in itself, designing it to fit the available space. Needless to say, the permanently attached unit is the cheapest to construct, under ordinary conditions. But, the most important point to remember is that house interior walls usually are not flat and the angles rarely a perfect 90 degrees. As a result no lines or measurements can be taken for granted and everything must be fitted individ-

ually. Thus, while considerable material is saved, much time is consumed in construction.

One of the most important operations in fitting the parts is "scribing." This consists of using a pair of dividers or compasses to trace the actual deviations of a wall from the perfectly flat and mark them upon the wood member that must rest against the surface. Actually, scribing is a simple matter of drawing one leg of the open dividers along the wall surface, while the other point moves along the top of the wood. This indicates directly on the edge of the wood the actual variations in the wall surfaces. If you then saw the wood along this line, the two surfaces will make contact the entire length of the wood. This is important in getting maximum support and rigidity from the member attached to the wall. The same system can be used to make skirts, or plinths to fit snugly to baseboards, etc.

Variations in angles have to be measured directly, and the piece made to conform instead of trying to force a right-angled frame into a corner several degrees out of square.

Equally important with these points is the proper attachment to structural members and not merely to plaster or wallboard surfaces. Conventional walls contain 2" x 4" studs spaced 19" apart on centers,

and it is to these studs that supporting parts of
the furniture should be attached. The location of
the stud can often be detected by tapping the wall,
and its presence verified by driving a thin finishing
nail through plaster and lath. The same method
can be used to find ceiling joists, but it is better
where possible to locate those joists from above and
poke a nail through along side the joist.

In attaching to brick or brick plastered over,
wood or fiber plugs should be used, inserted where
possible into the mortar joints. If screws are used,
so much the better. In hollow walls, where attachment cannot be made to studs, it may be possible
to employ toggle bolts. Here, especially, the structure must be solid and immovable so that there will
be no tugging or vibrating against the laths. Such

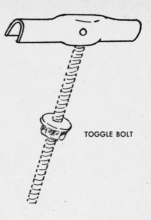

TOGGLE BOLT

stresses, especially those caused by swinging and
slamming doors, will bend the laths and crack the
plaster.

All of these built-in pieces call for something
much more than rough carpentry. The supporting
pieces should be of proper dimensions, planed
smooth, and fitted with precision. The joints, too,
should be those used in cabinet making, and the
parts put together in the same manner and with
equal care.

The ideal system therefore is to design the structure and plan the work so that much of it can be
done in the shop and only that necessary to fit it
to the space need be performed on the site. The
various pieces illustrated are designed with these
facts in mind.

RECESSED BOOKSHELF CUPBOARD

Figure I: One of the simplest of built-in units is
the bookshelf-cupboard applied to a doorway recess. Here you have the door frame to use as part
of the structure, though the door, if paneled, is
better replaced. In Fig. I such an arrangement is

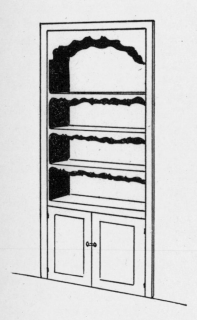

shown with all the new units inside the recess. The doorway has a simple architrave, though a more elaborate one might be just as successful. To get a maximum depth (8") and a plain back, the door has been replaced with a sheet of plywood. In other cases the paneled door might have a sheet of ¼" ply fastened over it to get the same effect. To ensure the least possible damage to the surround, the whole thing is lined with ⅝" boards which come within ⅝" of the face of the architrave. This lining consists of three pieces of ⅝" board assembled with the four shelves, the bottom one leaving space for the cupboard beneath it. The shelf measurements are made with the three pieces held tightly in position. With the lining pieces at the sides, the three upper shelves can have adjustable supports. The bottom one, forming the top of the cupboard, is best screwed to ¾" x ¾" supports. With the shelf section fitting snugly in the opening, the cut-out edges of the shelves and soffit and the rail over the doors are fitted exactly for width and fastened with finishing nails to the edges of the shelf and lining boards.

The door frame is completed with a pair of 1½" stiles on which the two doors are hung. These doors reach to the floor, but if the floor is too uneven to permit of them opening freely, a narrow rail also can be fitted across the bottom and the doors shortened to correspond.

to the shelves. Furthermore the 90-degree corner in the wall does not look well when framed by the woodwork. Much better appearance is secured by putting in a built-in wide board across that corner. If this is done, the shelves and their back boards can be assembled as a unit, and the front frame applied afterward. Exact fit therefore is most important for the shelf unit, but the front frame must

CORNER CUPBOARD

Figure II: A built-in corner cupboard, as shown, constitutes a slightly more complicated problem. Something fairly substantial is needed to secure the front stiles and the head. The long sides must be held firmly against the walls at all points, and this calls for a solid backing. Undoubtedly the best looking job is secured by providing a wooden back

be finished on the job to hide any discrepancies, and cut to fit any irregularities of the walls.

The entire back boarding and the four shelves can be constructed as a unit, and propped in position, and the facing boards then fastened to it. But these boards must have a flat surface to seat

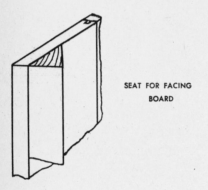

SEAT FOR FACING
BOARD

against. This is provided by beveling off the front edge of the back boards, and fastening triangular strips to them, about 2½ inches wide.

If the back boards are brought down to floor level, they can be trimmed so that the whole structure is a tight fit in the corner, and will need no further support than perhaps four nails, or screws, into the studs nearer the front edge.

The facing boards and arch are made in four pieces—two stiles carried up to the spring of the arch, and the arch cut in two at its vertical center. All these are simple flush butt joints, the upright edges being screwed to the triangular back strips. The center joint will call for a horizontal strip across the front of the inside assembly to which it can be firmly screwed. This member, possibly a 1" x 3", is let into the triangular side pieces and screwed into the edges of the back boards.

DOOR-FLANKING BOOKCASE

Figure III: A different set of problems is encountered in flanking a door with a pair of bookcases, as Fig. III. The whole structure is unified by carrying the frieze piece right across the doorway. The only drawback to this arrangement is that it tends to make a room look shorter. If this is objectionable, the center part of the frieze is best left out.

Apart from the frieze, this design consists of two separate but similar units built into two corners. Ordinarily, no wood back is needed. The walls form the back and one end of each, and only the inner end is of wood. In such a case it would be necessary to provide a strip down the angle of the wall to support the shelves, unless everything was attached directly to the walls. However, a much better arrangement is to install a board at both ends of the shelves, minimizing the danger to walls, and making the whole unit self-supporting. In a case like this you can make each set of shelves and end boards as a unit, place them in position, and then add the fascia board, stiles, and door frames. The end stiles are probably the only pieces that will have to be fitted to the walls by scribing. All four rails should be tenoned into the stiles, and these assembled and placed, temporarily, in position, before the frieze piece is cut out.

In most cases, the frieze, 10 inches or so deep, will have to be in more than one piece to span the room. In such a case the joint should be centered over one of the doorway stiles so that both boards can be nailed to the edge of the shelf end board. Any such joint should be well made so that it will not show through paint. For a stained job it might be better to make the frieze in three sections, with a joint over each doorway stile, and the grain matched accordingly. The joints between stiles and frieze can be fitted last, and trimmed to suit the ceiling irregularities. The doors are not made until the rest of the work is completed and finally installed.

THREE-UNIT COUNTER
AND CUPBOARD

Figure IV: The kitchen or living room fixture shown in Fig. IV is properly three units tied together with one continuous board forming the counter top. As usual in this semi-permanent form of construction, end boards are used, but no back, except for the center open-shelf section. As customary, the end stiles are cut to fit the walls exactly and measurements made while they are held in position. The counter board is neatly fitted and the top finished because that cannot readily be done later.

The end stiles are notched into the front of the board, and are continuous from floor to ceiling. Otherwise the section below the counter board and that above it are entirely separate. A small piece of nosing carried across the two end stiles makes it look as though the counter board separates them also. Note that the center portion of the counter board is cut back a couple of inches.

With the stiles and counter board cut, and dimensions taken, the rest of the work can be done in the shop. Construction is simplified if end boards are used, extending the full height of the cabinet, and fastened to the ends of the counter top. Otherwise a frame of square-section material (probably 2" x 2") will be necessary. The end boards should be dadoed for the counter top and the board that forms the floor of each cupbord.

The base is made first, with transverse boards separating the three sections. The cupboard rails are tenoned to the stiles and screwed to the counter top. In the end sections the stiles are fastened to the front edges of the transverse boards, and the stiles of the center section are screwed to those transverse boards farther back. When the base is finished as a unit, the upper sections are made.

The principal parts here, again, are the sides.

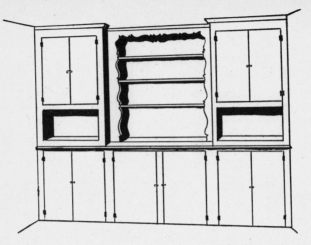

These two boards, reaching from the counter top to the ceiling, are dadoed for the cupboard bases. Both are set in position with the bases. Each cupboard frame is then assembled to the long stiles already in position and mortised for the horizontals. The fit to the ceiling here is not critical because an ogee or crown molding is used to cover that joint.

Finally, the cut-out frame of the center portion is made and mitered and trimmed down to fit snugly in the space. If a wooden back is used for the center section, it should be inserted first. The shelves in the center section are intended to be adjustable. Otherwise the inner sides of the end boards should be dadoed. The cut-out frame is best left plain, but may have its edges covered with a small moulding.

CLOSET AND
DRESSING TABLE ALCOVE

Figure V: This indicates a neat way of providing a bedroom closet by combining it with a dressing table alcove. Forming a complete unit across one wall, it does not appear to be an afterthought or a homemade addition. The main structure is a cupboard built on a pair of 2" x 2½" frames tenoned together. The top members are carried across the full width of the room, eight inches from the top of the uprights into which they are half-lapped. These terminate in another pair of uprights connected by transverse rails top and bottom. The whole system of 2 x 2½'s forms a rigid frame to which the facing boards are nailed or screwed. The bottom skirt board of the closet stiffens the whole door frame,

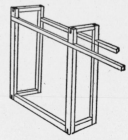

METHOD OF FRAMING

besides hiding the bottom 2" x 2½" rail by which
it is attached to the floor. This and the ceiling and
end boards may have to be scribed to the floor,
ceiling, and wall surfaces. The dressing table
counter is supported on cleats, and may have shelves
beneath it. Above is a large mirror. The cased
sides of this space may be cut away and recesses
provided for lights or shelves or both. The top
likewise can be cut away for a fluorescent tube,
either open or covered with ground glass. The door
surround should be rabbeted to keep out dust.

CORNER SEAT

Figure VI: A unit that is best built entirely into
the corner is the seat in Fig. VI. This unit is comparatively large and not likely to fit anywhere else.
Moreover, it must be quite rigid. The two end pieces
are made of heavy wood, two inches thick, and cut
out of one pieces. They can be dadoed for the
seat members, or have a cleat screwed to them. In
the former case, the seat support (a pair of 2" x 3"

CORNER SEAT DETAILS

longitudinals) would be tenoned into a short 2" x 3" which in turn would fit in the dado. This would be fastened with screws from the inside.

The seat frame would be made up of 2 x 3s, with another 2 x 3 running along the floor, a transverse stiffener and a pair of legs every four feet or so. The stiffener would be tenoned into the longitudinals, and the legs tenoned into the seat rail. The front leg would also tenon into the floor rail, but the rear one would rest on the floor and be carried up to form an attachment for the back rest.

At the seat corner, the two pairs of longitudinals would tenon into one another, with legs in each angle, and a back support. The back should have a slope for comfort. This can be provided by pieces sloping inward a couple of inches from the tops of the posts.

Details depend upon the method of upholstering. The seat and back can very well be covered with ⅜" to ⅝" plyboard, depending on the stiffness required. The front of the seat frame also could be boxed in with plywood, and it would add to comfort if it sloped inward a couple of inches toward the floor.

The back support can be either a sheet of plywood laid in at an angle behind the rear seat board, or composed of heavy supports attached to an upward extension of each rear leg, plus a top longitudinal. In the latter case webbing stretched between the supports, horizontally and vertically, would carry any upholstery. The alternative would be to pad the plywood.

In either case the top of the seat would be finished off with a strip of 1" x 2" with its front edge rounded completely off, as shown. This forms a capping for the legs and back board.

The most difficult part of this structure is the rounded corner. This calls for a top rail blocked out to take three pieces of plywood tapered toward the bottom. Padding on top of these changes the three flat surfaces into a continuous curve. If the webbing system is used, the corner can be filled in with a curved rail for the webbing attachment.

DOUBLE BUNKS, DETACHED

Figure VII: In contrast to the foregoing, the simplest type of built-in bed is that shown in Fig. VII Actually it is not built-in but is firmly attached because it is tall and cannot be taken apart. Normally such a bed, if 2' 6" wide or over, will stand of its own weight, especially if made of a heavy wood such as maple or oak. However, it can be made narrower with safety if attached in some manner to the floor or wall. The construction is obvious from the drawing, consisting of 3" x 3" legs,

with sides and ends of the bunks firmly tenoned in. A removable guard rail slips over the edge of the upper bunk. Slats are used to support the mattress. A much more ambitious form of this double bunk is that shown in Fig. VIII.

DOUBLE BUNKS, ATTACHED

Figue VIII: Here the whole frame is made of 1" x 3" boards, with lapped or rabbeted joints, strongly glued and screwed. The wider horizontal pieces are tenoned with the edges of the corner boards. These edges touching the ceiling can be scribed and shaped, but the corners in contact with the wall cannot. They need to be firmly screwed through to the wall studs after the complete strucure is assembled and fitted into position. A board forms the base of both beds. If laths are used, a strip of 1" x 1" can be inserted in each side corner to space them apart from the bottom board. This unit is intended to be painted all over so that no joints or end grain are visible.

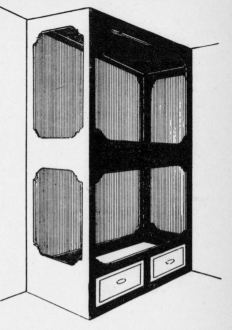

DIVAN WITH DRAWERS

Figure IX. For a bed-sitting room this divan serves a dual purpose, and is simple to make. The base consists of a box containing three drawers. The whole is made of ¾" boards. The top and bottom (made up of three boards glued together) are secret (lapped dovetailed into the ends, and the partitions tenoned into both. It will pay to make a

small lip all around the upper surface to hold the mattress or spring cushion in place.

If this unit is screwed to the floor, any skirting board should be removed first. Since the box portion is open at the back, the ends can be cut to fit over the baseboard. With no movement possible between the box and wall, no other support is needed for the cushions. But if the box is not attached, a light frame should be screwed to the back of it to hold the cushions while the piece is not in use as a bed.

CLOSET-BUNK-DESK

Figure X: This combined closet, bunk, and desk is built on the same principles as Fig. V, but the bed section will need a stiffer frame, say 2" x 3". Here, beveled t&g boards are used for facing. The

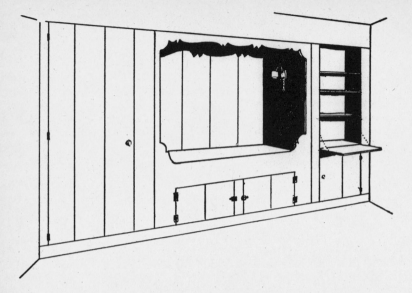

depth of the frieze board will depend upon the height of the room, but the head room over the bunk is best left open.

The main unit of the frame consists of the two transverse frames supporting the bottom of the bunk and joined by rails carrying it at the sides. All these joints are tenoned, and the uprights are let into horizontals, top and bottom, that go the full width of the room. Normally, the bunk would

not be more than 2' 6", back to front, but the desk shelves would be much shallower. This would leave a secret space behind the shelves which might be got at through a loose panel at the head of the bunk, or by doors in the backs of the shelves. With the substantial framing used, there need be few points of attachment to the walls, ceiling, and floor.

CABINET TABLE FOR CORNER BEDS

Figure XI: This illustrates a commonly used fixture that serves to fill in the corner space between two beds placed along adjacent walls. It is best made of plywood, but butt-jointed boards, glued, will do. Since the unit has no bottom it is easily assembled with screwed and glued corner blocks. The door hinges to the edge of the side and closes against the other edge, both edges being cut at 45 degrees to match the angle of the corner.

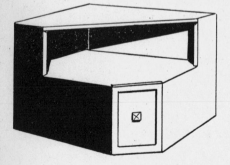

The two flat tops are let into the rabbeted edges of the sides and back. The lower top also is cut

LOWER TOP DETAIL—CABINET TABLE
FOR CORNER BEDS

away to fit tightly against the inner faces of the two partially open sides. If plywood is used, any end grain can be covered with flat strips of wood. The three edges visible around the open front should be so covered if they are plywood.

TWIN BEDS WITH BOOKSHELF-DESK

Figure XII: Twin beds can be made into a neat unit by a bookshelf-desk as in Fig. XII. This again is not strictly a built-in piece, though it should be firmly attached to the wall or floor. The bed units should be left free so that they can be swung aside

for making, etc. The treatment here is modern with no decoration, but with strict attention to proportion. The lower part of the unit can be cased in, or recesses may be made so that the heads of the beds can be pushed back into them. The small book or writing shelf is fixed, and a pair of gooseneck lamps built in for individual night reading. All is of ¾" lumber, the rails tenoned into the uprights, and the shelves and bottoms dadoed into the ends and partitions.

SOFA WITH BOOKCASE
AND END TABLES

Figure XIII: This is a somewhat similar device to Fig. XII, but adapted for a library or living room. The bookcase is shallow (seven inches or so) and carried on extensions of the end. In addition there are a pair of box-shaped ends in between which a sofa

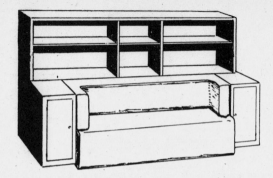

is intended to fit. These form end tables, and open in front as cupboards. Obviously, this piece must be built around some specific lounge or sofa, and the dimensions, particularly of the end pieces, must be determined by the bulk of the upholstered piece —they must not overpower it. Usually it is best, and most convenient, to make the shelves and ends separately, and secure them together below the bottom shelf and inside the ends, with detachable cleats.

WALL ANGLE CABINET
WITH DRAWERS

Figure XIV: This is essentially a kitchen piece, adapted from the Shakers, which fits into any wall angle. It is made almost entirely from ¾" boards, complete with back and bottom, but no top. The back can very well be of ⅜" matchboarding since it has no structural purpose. The horizontal drawer dividers and top are dovetailed into the center and end boards. The two vertical corner boards of the upper section are slightly rabbeted to take the end boards.

The bottom board, below the drawers, is dove-

tailed into the ends. Since there is no top to the cabinet, the inside angles of the front corners are best stiffened with long corner blocks, extending

from one shelf to the other, as well as above and below them. These shelves should be dovetailed in to help keep the upper section square and rigid.

CORNER COUNTER WITH
DROP TABLE

Figure XV: This is one corner of a kitchen counter with an idea for a drop table. Such counters, as a rule, need to be solidly built-in. They may be either framed or worked out of plywood or ¾" board. The best procedure is to set out the counter base, locating the partitions, and tying them together with fairly light longitudinals. The front bottom rail is set back a couple of inches to give toe room, and the drawers and bottom boards project level with the top rail. If the front and rear rails are connected by tenoned transverse rails, and the partitions set on these rails, there will be ample support on all sides for the bottom boards. The drop shelf shown is supported by a pair of butterfly brackets, hinged top and bottom to turn inwards. They are set far enough in so that the leaf fills the space without projecting beyond that point.

BATHROOM, KITCHEN
OR BAR COUNTER

Figure XVI: Bathroom counters, as in Fig XVI, are constructed on the same lines as the kitchen counter described above. A plywood top is an advantage in letting in the washbowl, some styles of which have flanges that must be set on, not in, the linoleum top. Finally there is the kitchen or bar counter that calls for a curved frame. This is usually open at the back and close-boarded in front. The principal part of the frame therefore is that supporting the boards on the outside curve.

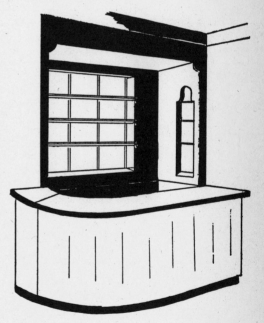

Several uprights are tenoned into 2" thick top and bottom rails. The curve is secured by making the rail from a wide piece of wood and curving that flat piece. The rails remain square but follow the line of the curve. The toe clearance is provided by mounting the bottom curved rail on a thicker rail made in sections and cut to the same curve. Fairly narrow and thin lapped boards are used to cover the front of the bar, and the top is made to project an inch or more beyond it.

Finishing Furniture

Chapter VI

Finishing Furniture

There are two general types of finishes, classified according to whether they are transparent or opaque. The transparent finishes, designed to bring out the natural beauty of the wood are oil, water, and spirit stains, rubbed oil and wax finishes, shellacs, varnishes, and clear lacquer. The opaque coatings include paint and lacquer enamels.

The most vital step in the finishing of furniture is the preparation of the wood surfaces. The wood is the foundation of the finish, and whether the finish is opaque or transparent, what lies under it will affect its character and reflect the degree of skill and care bestowed upon it.

In all newly made furniture, whether a copy of an old piece or the latest modern design, the basic treatment is the same. The wood must be smooth and free from rough grain, and all dust carefully wiped off before any finish is applied. The first stage in finishing any piece is the smoothing of the surface, and for this operation steel scrapers, sandpaper, and steel wool may be used.

Scraping

On certain woods, such as soft pines and cedar, it is sometimes advisable to smooth the surface after planing by scraping. The tool used is a flat piece of steel such as a piece, 5" x 2½", cut from a hand saw blade. The edge must be perfectly straight, and filed to a slight bevel, say 30 degrees, and smoothed on an oilstone. Then a cutting edge is formed on it by rubbing a piece of hard steel along the edge so that a burr is formed on one or both edges. The scraper is used by holding it firmly with both hands, bowing it slightly outward in the

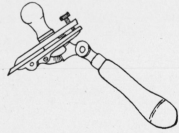

center and pushing (and sometimes pulling) it along parallel to the grain of the wood. The corners of the scraper should be rounded off so that they will not accidentally dig into the wood or scratch the surface. Curved scrapers can be used for hollow and rounded surfaces and for work on mouldings.

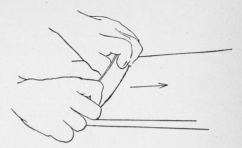

Sanding

The best type of sandpaper for fine cabinet work is the garnet paper, and the most useful grits are (in order of increasing coarseness) the 4/0, 3/0, 00, and 1/2. The 6/0, wet-or-dry paper, dipped in water, is often used for smoothing between finish coats. Sandpaper is always applied along the grain in a straight forward and back motion.

For flat surfaces the paper may be wrapped around a wood block. This helps to avoid ridges and keeps the paper from rubbing off the arrises and rounding the edges. No block is used in sanding rounded surfaces, though rounds or half-rounds may help in cleaning up some interior curves and the insides of holes.

Working with Steel Wool

Pads of steel wool can be used to finish any wood surface, though flecks of metal are apt to become imbedded. It is, however, better reserved for smoothing after the application of filler or the first coating. The coarsest wool used for these purposes is the No. 1; and Nos. 0 and 00 are generally better for fine work. In all cases the steel wool is applied in the direction of the grain. If a coating of any kind has been applied it is necessary to use long, sweeping, light strokes so as not to generate appreciable heat in any one spot.

Raising the Grain

For an extra-smooth surface it sometimes pays to raise the grain by slightly dampening, and sand off the swollen fibers after the surface has thoroughly dried. In administering this treatment, the very small amount of moisture required is best applied with a damp (not wet) cloth. After drying, the raised fibers can be smoothed off with No. 000 garnet paper applied with the hand (not with a block). Moisture can be used also to eliminate small nicks and dents. A folded wet cloth is held over the damaged area and heat is applied by means of a soldering bit or flat-iron. The steam generated swells the crushed or cut fibers, which are then allowed thoroughly to dry. Light sanding completes the operation.

The surfaces are finally prepared for the applied finish by removing all traces of dust and grease. This is best done by wiping gently with a rag slightly dampened with turpentine. Excess glue should be gently scraped off duirng final sanding.

Filling the Grain

All wood is porous to some degree, and if the grain is open, as in the case of oak, chestnut, walnut, mahogany, and cherry, a much smoother surface is secured by applying a special filler. It is also much simpler and cheaper to use a commercial filler of powdered quartz than to load the pores with paint, shellac, varnish, or lacquer.

The filler can be used either before or after the wood has been stained. If done before, the filler should be colorless; if applied after the stain, it should be the same color as the stain.

Sometimes a contrasting filler is used to get special effects with transparent finishes.

The fillers, which are usually mixed with linseed oil and a thinner such as turpentine, benzine, or naphtha, may need still further thinning before application. The filler is worked into the pores with a stiff-bristled brush, and, when almost dry, the excess is wiped off with burlap, across the grain. When dry, this surface may be cleaned with a soft cloth along the grain. A day later the surface can be smoothed with 00 steel wool. Since there is oil in the filler, it is advisable in the case of light-colored woods to give them a wash coat of thin, white shellac. This will prevent the oil from darkening the grain. Some finishers also use shellac as a sealer after filling.

Stains

Of the three types of stain available, the oil stain is much the best in the hands of a novice. The water stains raise the grain, and both they and the spirit stains are quite difficult to apply without streaking.

The oil stain should be applied with a clean varnish brush, after testing the color on a piece of scrap wood of the kind used in the furniture. If a light finish is required, the stain can be wiped off after a minute or so. The longer it is left, the darker it will become, within limits. If the stain is too dark to begin with, it may be thinned with turpentine. Since end grain absorbs more stain it normally finishes darker. This can be checked by dampening it with clear turpentine before staining.

In staining horizontal grains it is usual to begin in the center and work toward the ends. For vertical grain, as in cabinet ends, start at the top and work down. Any recesses or inside angles should be done first, but do not let any part dry before completing the whole surface.

The use of a water stain calls for a preliminary dampening, drying and finish sanding of the wood to forestall any raising of the grain by the stain. To the novice it may be easier to apply the stain with a spray gun, though even that is not proof against unevenness. If a brush is used it should be a fairly large one, and the stain applied rapidly because it is so quickly absorbed by the wood. Excess stain would be wiped off each surface as it is completed, and any lap marks may be toned down by going over the whole surface with a dry brush. The excessive darkening of end grain can be controlled by dampening it first with water or lightly brushing with glue size. Most of the water stains need to be freshly mixed a short time before use, preferably in slightly warm water.

In spirit stains the solvent is alcohol, and the rapid evaporation makes it difficult to apply the color evenly. Otherwise the method of application is the same as for water stains, though no preliminary dampening or sanding is necessary.

Clear Finishes

One of the most satisfactory finishes that does not change the natural color of the wood is white shellac. Afer filling the wood grain, if necessary, several coats of clear shellac are applied. The first coat needs to be thinned by adding ½ gal. alcohol to 1 gal. of 4-lb.-cut shellac. Succeeding coats should have less thinner, and the final one is the full 4-lb. strength. Three or four coats should be sufficient, with a light sanding with 006 garnet paper between applications. The surface can later be protected and given a pleasing deep gloss with a coat of wax, well rubbed.

Varnish will give an even richer finish than shellac though it may darken the wood a little. It takes more care and effort to do a varnishing job because of the length of time the surface remains soft and picks up dust. A dust-free room kept at a temperature of about 70 degrees F. is the first requirement. Either a glossy or dull-finish varnish can be used. A dull finish can be given to a glossy varnish by rubbing with steel wool or pumice. The varnish can be used over a surface sealed with shellac, and each coat allowed to dry overnight. Some varnishes need 72 hours to dry. Before applying the next coat, always test the last one by pressing with the fingernail. If this makes an impression, the coat is not dry.

Between each coat rub down the varnish lightly with 6/0 garnet paper or 2/0 steel wool along the grain, and wipe off with a clean, soft rag. A final coat of wax can be applied if desired.

Lacquer forms an excellent transparent surface that will stand abuse, but it is best applied with a spray gun. Some slow-drying lacquers have been developed for brushing. They may or may not have solvents that enable them to be used over other finishes. Lacquer dries quickly and so is not so likely to pick up dust. Three coats should be applied, and sanding is not necessary because one coat softens and unites with the coat underneath. Either glossy or flat lacquers can be procured to give any required finish.

Bleaching

To get a light finish on dark woods, or to remove dark streaks from light woods, a bleaching process is necessary. Streaks on light wood can often be touched up with a strong, hot solution of oxalic acid in water. The acid must then be "killed" by applying an alkaline solution, such as soda or borax. For bleaching the dark woods a more powerful bleach is required. Such bleaches can be obtained from most paint stores with full directions for their use. All bleaches raise the grain, and should be followed by careful sanding.

Various types of blond finishes can be applied to the bleached wood. Most of them use a natural-color, or slightly tinted filler. A number of commercial finishes are available to simulate the transparent finishes on surfaces that have been finished in some other way. For example blond maple or limed oak can be simulated by applying first a ground color over which a graining compound is brushed, then

wiped off with cheese cloth. The final coat is a clear lacquer.

Opaque Finishes

For finishes that hide the grain of the wood there is a wide choice of opaque lacquers, enamels, and paints. These can all either be left plain or decorated by stenciling, transfers (decalcomanias), or free-hand painted designs. The pigmented lacquers need to be sprayed, but enamels with synthetic bases can be brushed on. With enamels the best results are obtained by priming soft woods with thin shellac, and heavily grained woods with thinned varnish enamel or a special undercoater. For dark woods this undercoater can be tinted to the approximate final color. Two coats of enamel are usually sufficient, with a light sanding between applications.

Toning and Antiquing

Light woods newly finished have a pristine air that sets them apart from older furntiure that they are used alongside. This "sore thumb" effect may not always be desirable and it sometimes helps to tone down the new finish. This is quite simple, particularly on pieces that have a shellac finish. All that is required is a thin paint wash made up of about three parts burnt umber and one part burnt sienna, oil colors. These are well diluted in turpentine, with a few drops of japan drier added. This is mixed to a thin creamy consistency and brushed over the entire surface to be treated.

In a few minutes, when this coating shows signs of drying, almost all of it should be wiped off. The wiping must be carefully done, in the direction of the grain, using very soft rags with no hard folds or seams. If this is done properly, all the wood grain will be exposed, but the whole surface will have a soft warm tone. Highlight effects can be obtained by wiping over the edges and high spots a second time.

The finish should not be streaky, and if the first attempt is not successful, the paint can be wiped off, and a new attempt made. This finish is left to dry for 72 hours, and can then be waxed as usual. If a hard wearing surface is needed, as in table tops, this toning can be varnished over in the regular way. For furniture that is to be antiqued the same system is used, but a little more color left on. The surface is then waxed with a wax darkened with some of the same paint mixture.

Designing Furniture

Chapter VII

Designing Furniture

It is interesting to plan an odd piece for some special location or to serve some particular purpose, and, in the case of built-in units, it is nearly always necessary to plan or lay out the parts or units for the best effect. The aim should be to secure results that combine good workmanship with nice proportion and beauty of line. The essentials of good workmanship are sound construction and first-class finish, to professional standards. Sound construction involves accurate and strong jointing and design that ensures a proper distribution of stresses. Nice proportion demands a careful balancing of masses so that the piece does not look top-heavy or lopsided, or awkward. In some modern pieces, however, top-heaviness may be excused, as when a case piece is mounted on spidery legs simply because those legs are of iron and therefore recognizably strong in proportion to the weight of the wooden section. Such design usually are best left to the professional designer, but in all respects well-designed furniture must *appear*, as well as *be*, wholly adapted to the purpose it is to serve. Appearance is important, and second only to utility. The degree to which the two can be combined is a measure of the designer's taste and skill. But it should be remembered that any well-designed piece looks like what it is and not like something else.

Don't make a piece till you have drawn it to a fairly large scale. This will give you an idea of its final appearance, perhaps from the front and one side. Pay special attention to the joints—the potential weak spots—in deciding upon the principal dimensions. There should be no great or sudden change in sectional area, and top-heavy effects are to be avoided.

Woods such as mahogany and birch are stronger than white pine or whitewood and therefore can be used in pieces of more delicate proportions. Oak, in particular, looks best in pieces of sturdy design, while tough stock such as ash is more logically used for spindles and parts that may be expected to "give" than is a brittle wood like mahogany.

These characteristics of the various woods also need to be taken into consideration in decorating them. Simple pieces need but simple embellishments; you want no fancy curves or curlicues on pine pieces—simple chamfers, dentils, comparatively coarse mouldings, and no sharp arrises, and only simple designs in chisel and gouge work should be attempted. The finer and denser the wood the more complicated and delicate the decoration can be.

In designing special pieces it is usually simplest

170

to copy or adapt existing pieces that are of accepted good design, either of classical or modern styles. Even here it is necessary to exercise both taste and judgment. In copying or adapting modern pieces it is much more essential to use discrimination or restraint, and you should have at least an elementary knowledge of design principles. Furniture that is to be lived with should not be extreme or freakish either in design or decoration. If you decide to copy existing pieces be sure that they are worth reproducing both from a design and appearance standpoint, and are in good taste. As a rule, you will need to copy them exactly as to size as well as proportion. Some pieces that look well in their original size are much less admirable when built to a larger or smaller scale.

In the case of upholstered pieces it should be remembered that good design may be spoiled by the use of poorly designed or unsuitable fabrics. The covering should always contribute to the design and not detract from it, and it should match the woodwork in delicacy or ruggedness of "feel." A vast amount of ill-designed furniture has appeared on the market since mass-production methods were adopted by the industry. On the other hand there are so many excellent examples of really well-made and tasteful furniture available that there is neither need nor excuse for perpetuating these errors.

Taste is a prime factor in determining the merit of a piece of furniture. To be in good taste, a piece should be of nice proportions and design, suited to its purpose, not over-decorated or flamboyant in style, nor flashy in finish. The material should also be suited to the design. A highly decorative wood, for example, is not particularly suited to kitchen furniture, and a design that calls for surface decoration may look far better executed in a plain, straight-grained wood than a fancy one.

Use also affects suitability. Few people in the USA would approve of mahogany kitchen furniture, though it would not look so strange in tropical countries where is it commonly found. Furniture for strenuous everyday use needs to be of far more rugged design than that used in places where appearance takes precedence over utility.

When hand-made furniture gave way largely to machine products, design often had to be modified to permit of mass manufacture. In many instances design suffered because the little refinements and manifestations of careful hand work were lost. Many modern furniture designs have been introduced, some of them frankly experimental, but most of them intended to take full advantage of machine production while minimizing the effects of its limitations. In many instances this has resulted in a sharp breaking away from traditional design, but in some important exceptions the adaptations of the hand-made pieces have proved equally as attractive as the originals. In other cases, equivalent results have been achieved by hand-finishing the machine products.

Paralleling this development has been the introduction and use of formerly rare and exotic woods and modern finishes that entirely alter the characteristic appearance of the commoner woods. Many designs have been developed to take advantage of the special characteristics of these woods (grain, color, and surface texture), and combinations of contrasting woods. For example, a particularly attractive cabinet can be made in light mahogany veneer, with front panels of olive-figure ash and Bombay rosewood.

Mahogany in the modern light finish is popular in many pieces, as is beech. These blond woods lend themselves very well to use with a wide variety of fabric colors and designs, and sometimes with table tops or cabinet fronts of brightly colored plastics.

In all these adaptations and combinations of materials the important thing is to avoid any suggestion of cheapness, sloppy workmanship, or crudity. The design must be good, and carried out

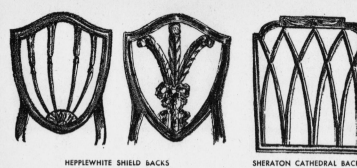

HEPPLEWHITE SHIELD BACKS   SHERATON CATHEDRAL BACKS

PHYFE   SHERATON

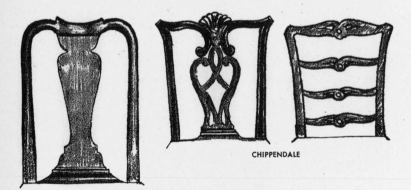

QUEEN ANNE   CHIPPENDALE

SOME TRADITIONAL CHAIRBACK DESIGNS

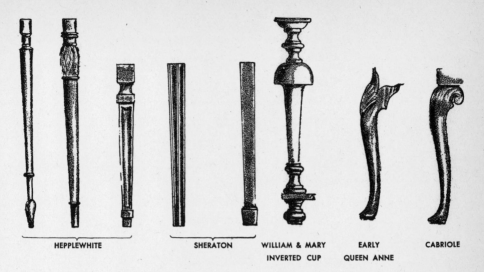

| HEPPLEWHITE | SHERATON | WILLIAM & MARY INVERTED CUP | EARLY QUEEN ANNE | CABRIOLE |

with a high degree of skill and care. You cannot take liberties with these products of modern master-designers, any more than you can with the fine old traditional pieces, and expect happy results. Where line and proportion, color and texture are all vital components of a design, you need to give the whole piece careful study. And you need to know something of design yourself before tampering with it. Therefore, if you copy any of the recognizedly acceptable pieces, old or new, copy them as exactly as you can.

In that way you will gradually learn to detect and appreciate the elements of good design and how to incorporate them in any original piece you attempt yourself.

Gone about in a proper manner, the designing of a piece of furniture for your purpose can be as exciting and satisfying as painting a picture. When once you have grasped the essentials of design, the rest is merely a matter of patient concentration in laying out the design on paper.

Rough out the shape of the principal parts to scale on squared paper. Then, when you are satisfied with the general proportions you can transfer

HEPPLEWHITE DECORATIONS—PRINCE OF WALES FEATURES, SWAG, BELLFLOWER HUSKS

the outlines of the various units to a large sheet of drawing paper at as nearly full scale as convenient. This enables you to visualize the shapes of the parts and their actual proportions and relationships to one another, and to experiment with the curves and joint angles.

When you are satisfied with the actual shapes and proportions of the various parts, you can make a complete scale drawing showing them assembled. Finally, the details of the parts can be transferred at full size to sheets of brown paper to be used as working drawings or even cut out as patterns.

If you are dealing with a bulky piece such as a set of shelves and cupboards (a shallow cabinet without legs), a moderately large scale drawing, showing the proportions and relationship of the divisions or units from the front, may be sufficient. In such a case it is as well to shade the enclosed parts (i.e., those having doors or panels) to give a more solid effect for comparison with open parts, such as shelves, which do not seem so heavy in the finished job.

Modular Furniture

Modular furniture is furniture designed to conform to architectural conceptions of mass and form. The furniture pieces are made to certain standard sizes and proportions, multiples of the unit size or module, and when assembled in a room should produce the effect of architectural balance. In many designs, two or more of the unit pieces can be assembled to serve different purposes. For example, small cubic tables can be put together in twos or threes to make end tables, or assembled in a row as a cocktail table.

It is quite easy to adapt this principle to the design of a piece of furniture that can be progressively altered to suit changing conditions. For example, you might start with a top and base of a fairly large cabinet, and fit between them a pair of small cupboards. These might be placed at the

ends of the base to leave an open storage space between them. The next stage of the project might be to move the two cabinets together in the center, and add a narrower cabinet at each end, these having doors in their ends—or one of them might be equipped with drawers. This is a simple example of how such a piece might be designed and then built and finally assembled in stages.

Sectional upholstered pieces likewise are made that can be used as separate chairs and stools or to form a complete sofa. All of these and similar pieces are interesting to the home furniture maker because of the variations they permit in furniture arrangement. Today much furniture is planned carefully to serve one or more purposes, since modern homes, in the aggregate, are smaller and need more services, and therefore increased flexibility in

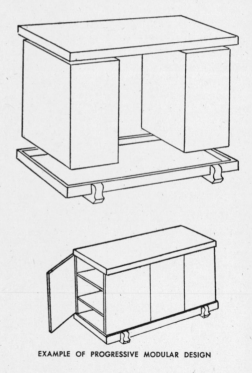

EXAMPLE OF PROGRESSIVE MODULAR DESIGN

furniture arrangements. One designer has developed 12 basic shape units from which 150 different pieces of furniture can be assembled. Other have designed standard units with various bases and tops that permit varied grouping and completely change the appearance of the original basic pieces. Many such pieces are now available and can be examined in the larger stores by anyone interested. For the home craftsman the modular system offers a challenge to develop designs of his own.

Appendix

Appendix

Cabinet Hardware Manufacturers

Period Furniture Hardware Co., 123 Charles Street, Boston, Mass.

Russel & Erwin Mfg. Co., New Britain, Conn.

Old Guilford Forge, Guilford, Conn.

Ball & Ball, Inc., Whitford, Pa.

The Stanley Works, New Britain, Conn.

Ball Brasses, West Chester, Pa.

Tool Makers

Adjustable Clamp Co., Chicago 22, Ill. (Jorgensen).

North Bros. Mfg. Co., (Division of Stanley Tools), Philadelphia 33, Pa.

Henry Disston & Sons, Inc., Tacony, Philadelphia, Pa.

Stanley Electric Tools, New Britain, Conn.

Delta Mfg. Division, Rockwell Mfg. Co., Milwaukee 1, Wis.

Finishing Material Manufacturers

H. Behlen & Bros. 10 Christopher Street, New York 14, N. Y.

The Savogran Co., Boston, Mass.

Boston Varnish Co., Boston, Mass.

Devoe & Reynolds Co., Inc., New York.

Wilson-Imperial Co., 123 Chestnut Street, Newark 5, N. J.

Murphy Paint Division, Interchemical Corp., New York.

Ordinary Nail Sizes

Size	2d	3d	4d	5d	6d	7d	8d	9d	10d
Length	1"	1¼"	1½"	1¾"	2"	2¼"	2½"	2¾"	3"
No. per lb.	900	615	322	254	200	154	106	85	74

Screw Sizes

Lengths Size No.	0	1	2	3	4	5	6	7	8	9	10	11	12
¼ in.	x	x	x	x	x								
⅜ "		x	x	x	x	x	x	x	x	x	x		
½ "		x	x	x	x	x	x	x	x	x	x	x	x
⅝ "		x	x	x	x	x	x	x	x	x	x	x	x
¾ "			x	x	x	x	x	x	x	x	x	x	x
⅞ "			x	x	x	x	x	x	x	x	x	x	x
1 "				x	x	x	x	x	x	x	x	x	x
1¼ "				x	x	x	x	x	x	x	x	x	x
1½ "					x	x	x	x	x	x	x	x	x
1¾ "					x	x	x	x	x	x	x	x	x
2 "					x	x	x	x	x	x	x	x	x
2¼ "					x	x	x	x	x	x	x	x	x
2½ "						x	x	x	x	x	x	x	x
2¾ "						x	x	x	x	x	x	x	x
3 "						x	x	x	x	x	x	x	x
3½ "									x	x	x	x	x
4 "									x	x	x	x	x

Note: Above are sizes most commonly used in cabinet making and for built-ins. Other sizes are available—larger.

TYPICAL FURNITURE SIZES

Tables

Dining: 32-in. high.
Coffee: 16-20-in. high (extreme: 12-in).
Occasional: 27-in high.
Side: 30-in. high.
Typing: 25-in. high.
Work: 28-in. high.
Writing: 30-in. high.
Bedside: 30-in. high.
Kitchen: 31-in. high.
Candle stand: 27-in. high.

Chairs

Dining: 18-in. high seat.
Bedroom: 14-in. high seat(upholstered).
Lounge: 15-in. high seat (upholstered).
Desk: 16½-in. high seat (upholstered).
Seats
  Sofa: 16-18-in. high seat (upholstered).
  Ottoman: 14-16-in. high seat (upholstered).

Beds

Side rail: 14-in. high, 6 ft 6-in. long.

Cabinets

Kitchen (floor) 34-in. x 24-in. deep.
Kitchen (wall) 30-in. high.
Bathroom: 19-20-in. high.
Record: 36-in. high.
Corner or square: Base 38-in. Top 42-in. high.
Vanity dresser: 28-in. high.
Buffet: 30-in. high.
Reading desk: 30-in. high (dictionary stand, etc.).
Dressing chest: 48-in. high.
Sideboard: 34-in. high.
Bathroom hamper: 25-in. high.